REIGN OF THE
ANUNNAKI

REIGN OF THE ANUNNAKI

The Alien Manipulation of Our Spiritual Destiny

JAN ERIK SIGDELL

Bear & Company
Rochester, Vermont

Bear & Company
One Park Street
Rochester, Vermont 05767
www.BearandCompanyBooks.com

Bear & Company is a division of Inner Traditions International

Originally published in 2016 in German under the title *Die Herrschaft der Anunnaki: Manipulatoren der Menschheit für die Neue Weltordnung* by AMRA Verlag & Records, Auf der Reitbahn 8, D-63452 Hanau, Germany, translated and reedited by the author.
First U.S. edition published in 2018 by Bear & Company

Library of Congress Cataloging-in-Publication Data
Names: Sigdell, Jan Erik, 1938– author.
Title: Reign of the Anunnaki : the alien manipulation of our spiritual destiny / Jan Erik Sigdell.
Other titles: Herrschaft der Anunnaki. English
Description: Rochester, Vermont : Bear & Company, 2018. | Includes bibliographical references and index.
Identifiers: LCCN 2017058343 (print) | LCCN 2018016156 (ebook) | ISBN 9781591433033 (pbk.) | ISBN 9781591433040 (ebook)
Subjects: LCSH: Mythology, Sumerian. | Mythology, Assyro-Babylonian. | Civilization, Ancient—Extraterrestrial influences. | Extraterrestrial beings. | Gnosticism—History.
Classification: LCC BL1615 .S5413 2018 (print) | LCC BL1615 (ebook) | DDC 001.942—dc23
LC record available at https://lccn.loc.gov/2017058343

Printed and bound in the United States by Versa Press, Inc.

10 9 8 7 6 5 4 3 2 1

Text design and layout by Virginia Scott Bowman
This book was typeset in Garamond Premier Pro and Frutiger with Andea used as the display typeface.

To send correspondence to the author of this book, mail a first-class letter to the author c/o Inner Traditions • Bear & Company, One Park Street, Rochester, VT 05767, and we will forward the communication.

CONTENTS

THE ORIGINS OF HUMANITY AND ITS RELIGIONS

Much has been said about the Anunnaki today. They are mentioned in ancient Mesopotamian writings, as well as in the contexts of esotericism and fringe science. They also feature in the volatile topic of the New World Order as it relates to politics and global issues. It is astonishing—at least for those who have not dealt with the hidden history of our world—to discover how all these things interweave. But who are the Anunnaki? Do they really exist? What sources tell us anything about them? Is there a planet Nibiru?

SITCHIN, TELLINGER, AND PARKS

The subject gained attention through the books of Zecharia Sitchin (1920–2010), who set forth the theory that the Anunnaki are visitors to our Earth from a planet named Nibiru. Sitchin's books and hypotheses met with much interest but were criticized by scientists and skeptics. He was reproached for giving too few references to sources for his interpretations of Mesopotamian texts. It was also claimed that his linguistic interpretations were amateurish. It is true that his source references are much too few, and the question about his linguistic qualifications may be justified. Nevertheless, his theses are remarkable, even if they are only partially correct (though these may be essential parts). (As a kind of response to repeated questions about sources, Sitchin published *The Lost Book of Enki* in 2004. It gives the impression of a real Mesopotamian document but raises more questions since no source at all is stated, and some have, therefore, assumed it to be a construction.)

Michael Tellinger carries Sitchin's theses further in his interesting book *Slave Species of the Gods*, and he corroborates them with his own investigations and comparisons with various cultures. In my view, however, Tellinger relies too uncritically on Sitchin's writings, especially *The Lost Book of Enki*. His opinions about Jesus and Christ as agents of the Anunnaki derive from a layman's view of ecclesiastical Christianity. If he had engaged more critically in the history of Christianity and especially of Gnostic Christianity, he could not have written as he did. As a result, his claims about Jesus are erroneous. As I will show here, Jesus was a messenger of Christ and had the mission of informing us about the rule of the Anunnaki: that was why he was killed. This mission was carried on by the Gnostic Christians until they too were eliminated by the ruling powers. Another problem with Tellinger's text is that it lacks direct references to sources: there is only a general bibliography.

Later, another writer joined the discussion. The French-German author Anton Parks published some books in French, of which *Eden: La vérité sur nos origines* (Eden: The truth about our origins) is the most important. Parks translates Mesopotamian texts quite differently from previous linguists and ethnologists.

Although the result is an interesting contribution to the subject, it contains some surprisingly erroneous linguistic references to Hebrew concepts. Moreover, as I will explain later, some of his assertions can be questioned. Again, source references are sparse, especially concerning Mesopotamian texts. He cites only coded notations for cuneiform texts, making it difficult to compare his translations with others.

SO WHO ARE THEY?

Why are they called Anunnaki? This word means *the people of Anu,* and it first appeared in Mesopotamia on cuneiform clay tablets that are several thousand years old. In this book, I will retell and discuss the story of the Anunnaki according to these tablets. This is done from more of a spiritual viewpoint, in contrast to the common, and rather dry, scientific attitude, which is based on a limited worldview.

The traditional approach to creation myths is to regard them as such—as myths—but we will consider them under the hypothesis that they may have a factual background. What does this hypothesis mean for our monotheistic religions, and what worldview will that lead to? Moreover, what connections could there be with actual occurrences in our world?

I will try to give answers that will probably not appeal immediately to all readers, depending on their worldviews, but at any rate will offer material for discussion and reflection. My intention is to span a bridge between, on the one hand, the common "scientific" views on this subject, and, on the other hand, the numerous esoteric books and ideas, which have their defects as well. The latter in many cases lack a proper grounding in the clay tablets and other ancient texts, and sometimes provide isolated quotations that do not stand up to verification.

A first millennium Mesopotamian cylinder seal impression.
This image—in the conventional interpretation—shows a worshipper
and a fish-garbed sage, with a stylized tree and a crescent moon
and winged disk above it. To the left is the dragon of Marduk, with
Marduk's spear and Nabu's standard on its back. Some of these
elements will be discussed later in this text.

ARE THERE REALLY EXTRATERRESTRIALS?

The widespread opinion that the Anunnaki belonged to an extraterrestrial race is, of course, taboo in circles that consider themselves scientific. Yet if we study the Mesopotamian texts, we will not find contradictions to this interpretation: it is logically possible. It merely conflicts with the present-day official worldview and the customary dogmatism found in "scientific" circles.

Today it should be clear that we cannot possibly be alone in the universe. Mainstream astronomy now estimates that there are trillions of planets in the cosmos, and the probability that only one of them has biological life is almost zero. Since there are probably hundreds of thousands of populated planets, it is also probable that other civilizations are out there.

ORIGINS OF RELIGIONS

The present treatise is based on research into the history of religions and looks ahead in connection with spiritual and esoteric sources. Unlike the above-mentioned works, it cites a large number of sources that can be found in relevant books and on the internet. I will avoid attempting a scientific transliteration of words from non-European languages.* Please note also that I will not distinguish strictly among the various cultures in question but will for the most part use the general term *Mesopotamian.* As for the many links to the internet that are cited, a number of them will no longer be available after some time, because the URLs will change or the websites will no longer be active. I hope that the interested reader will be able to find corresponding websites with the help of the information that is given.

■ ■ ■

I would also like to express my thanks to Jennie Marx of Inner Traditions/Bear & Company for her suggestions and helpful editing of the text.

---

*I, however, usually use the symbols ' to denote the Hebrew letter *aleph* and ' to denote the letter *ain,* since this is helpful for finding corresponding words in a Hebrew dictionary. Many texts simply leave these out.

1

THE ANUNNAKI
AND THE CREATION
OF HUMANITY

*Facts about Us in
the Mesopotamian Clay Tablets*

The ancient Mesopotamian cultures consisted of Sumer (3500–1800 BCE), Akkad (2340–2125 BCE), Babylonia (2000–1000 BCE), and Assyria (1170–612 BCE). (These are all approximate dates and vary somewhat from one source to another.)

These civilizations left a large number of texts in cuneiform writing on clay tablets. Many of these have been preserved to this day, even though some are damaged or broken; others have no doubt been stolen and are now in private possession or kept at unknown locations. Regrettably, some have even appeared to be used as building material for houses. It was only in the nineteenth century that these texts could gradually be deciphered and the valuable clay-tablet literature became accessible. With this, a worldview appeared that had previously been unknown in modern times.

Among the most important texts in our context is the Babylonian creation story *Enuma Elish* (so called after its first two words, which mean "when above"), written on seven tablets, which gives some information about the creation of humans.[1] I will briefly describe this creation story, referring to various translations (which differ in part, in some cases extensively). A much older description is published in another of my books, *Es begann in Babylon* (It began in Babylonia).[2] This book was published in 2008; today I would have written much of it quite differently.

Early scholars dated the *Enuma Elish* to about 2000 BCE. Some more recent authors want to date it some one thousand years later. A more accurate dating remains uncertain.

Official science regards these stories as tales and mythologies without any correspondence to the actual cosmos. Because there are remarkable parallels to the first books in the Old Testament, especially Genesis, one would logically have to also regard the latter as pure mythology (as some actually do). As a result, I will write using the equally admissible hypothesis that the Mesopotamian stories may also be based upon actual truths.

The *Enuma Elish* tells us that the Goddess Tiamat was the primordial mother of the race of the gods.* Their primordial father was Apsu, her male partner. Out of their union a kind of personified power of creation emerged, called Mummu. They mixed their energies, and three generations of gods came to be. The first of these was the divine pair Lahmu and Lahamu, out of which emerged Anshar and Kishar. A third generation followed: the one of the heavenly god Anu, with two female mates, and their sons Enlil ("lord of the storm") and Enki ("lord of the Earth," also

---

*I will generally write the term *god* and *gods* with a lowercase g and will spell *God* with a capital G only when it refers to real Creators, that is, to Apsu, Tiamat, and Christian concepts of a real Creator (except for Yahweh, for reasons I will explore in this book).

Enlil, Lord of the Storm

A detail from the Adda Seal showing Enki, center, with streams of
water and fish flowing from his shoulders.

called Ea or Nudimmud), who also had their female companions. Out of them, a race of gods then emerged, called Anunnaki or Anunna.

After they had emerged, the divine brothers, Enlil and Enki, and the other Anunnaki disturbed Apsu and Tiamat with their behavior. Although Apsu could not pacify them, Tiamat was tolerant at first. Then Apsu called his counselor or vizier, Mummu. They went to Tiamat to get her advice. They actually wanted to exterminate these divine brothers, or rather reverse their creation. Tiamat was infuriated, because she was their primal mother, and she wanted to discipline them benevolently. Mummu, however, advised Apsu to continue with the extermination, and Apsu was pleased.

We will have to understand Apsu in two ways. In one aspect, he is the primordial energy out of which the creation came to be, but in another aspect he is also that energy as a personified entity. Tiamat is often characterized as another primordial energy but can also be understood as an entity representing the female (birth-giving) part of an androgynous aspect of *one* Creator.* These entities are often devalued when it does not fit the common worldview to see them as Gods.

Enki discovered their plans and thwarted them. Using spells, he put Apsu and Mummu to sleep, stripped Apsu of the signs of

---

*Tiamat and Apsu are often described as waters of a primordial sea, and translators use such expressions as *seawater*, *sweet water*, and *abyss* to refer to them. But these ideas were generated by ethnologists with a purely materialistic worldview and lacking an understanding of spiritual levels of existence. What is called *water* in translations has to do with *energetic realms* beyond our three-dimensional world, a concept that was inconceivable to earlier (as well as to some contemporary) ethnologists. Tiamat is also sometimes characterized as a chaos monster. In my opinion, this has to do with the fact that, in her fight with Marduk, she had to defend herself and thus needed to create horrible weapons that appeared as monsters (which I will describe below). Tiamat is also characterized as a woman, with a motherliness that does not give the impression of a monster.

his power, and killed him. Mummu was fettered. Enki had won and established a world "on Apsu" to which he gave the Creator's name—meaning that he built his own world on the basis of the already existing creation. Thus Enki hijacked a part of the primordial energy. The sphere of life and power of Enki was now called Apsu. Here the god Marduk, the wisest of the wise, was born of Enki and his female partner Damkina (also called Damgalnuna). This god, who had four eyes and four ears, was to become the destroyer of Tiamat, and he molested her day and night with "waves," also translated as *streams, wild surf,* or *flood waves* (and, improbably, in one German translation as "reed swamp," which can hardly reflect the energetic nature of the attack).

Some of the gods now have evil plans. They accuse Tiamat of passivity and challenge her to fight. Tiamat prepares herself. The gods split: some support Marduk, and some take the side of Tiamat, who had previously given birth to them. Tiamat produces invincible weapons such as monstrous snakes, with sharp teeth and bodies filled with poison, for her defense in the coming confrontation. She manifests cruel but godlike dragons, who raise fear at the mere sight of them. A horde of monsters is assembled—a hydra dragon, a demon (also called Lahamu), a rabid dog, a lion man, a scorpion man, tempest demons, and so on. Eleven kinds of monsters arise, and Tiamat's firstborn Kingu ("laborer") becomes their leader as well as Tiamat's new spouse. In this, we may see a separation of the originally unified energies of Apsu and Tiamat.

Enki finds out about these preparations and feels afraid. He informs Anshar, who is also greatly disturbed, and asks Enki to appease Tiamat. Since Enki has already killed Apsu, Anshar wants him to kill Kingu also. He is aware of Tiamat's strength and asks him to send another against her. Anshar then turns to Anu, who first wants to negotiate with Tiamat but then shrinks back as a result of her preparedness to fight. The Anunnaki—the people of

Anu—are alarmed. Enki now calls Marduk to his chamber and orders him to fight, and he accepts the task with bellicosity.

Marduk approaches Tiamat, with all of his assisting gods marching at his side. Tiamat roars vehemently, and Marduk accuses her of having caused conflict in arrogance and pride and of having aroused discord through conspiracy. Sons would have done injustice to their fathers because of her influence, and she would have groundlessly hated her own children. She would have sought evil. Marduk turns the tables. He challenges her to a fight that ends with her death.

Now it is obviously impossible that Marduk and his cohort could have killed the primordial Creators and destroyed all the cosmos therewith: it would have meant suicide for themselves. Therefore the true meaning is that they turned their back on the Creators and declared them as dead to the Anunnaki: the latter would live as if the Creators no longer existed. In that way, they made a separate region in the universe for themselves, a kind of enclave in which they lived as if they were alone. Hence—if we are to assume a basic reality behind the story rather than regarding it as only a myth—we can also assume that there are other regions in the universe besides the Anunnaki enclave. This would explain the existence of other divine beings (or extraterrestrials) that are not mentioned in the clay-tablet texts and that were probably unknown to the Mesopotamians.

GOOD AND EVIL
IN THE DIVINE WORLD

The first impression we get is that there were "black sheep" among the gods that emerged from Apsu and Tiamat. In a motherly way, Tiamat wanted to tolerate them, but Apsu wanted to eliminate them so as to restore order and peace. The troublemakers then carried out a revolution and took power through violence and murder. (This resembles the familiar story about Satan and the fallen angels who followed him.) Tiamat, convinced of the need to fight, prepared to intervene and defend herself.

Which side is evil then? On the one hand, the texts mention the "evil plan" of Mummu and Apsu for doing away with the "divine troublemakers," and it is written that Tiamat "contemplated the evil in her heart" (other, remarkably different, translations are "grieved in her heart," "suppressed the evil in her belly," "despaired about the evil plans," and "uttered a curse") when she first rejected this plan. On the other hand, Enki murders his grandfather and has his grandmother killed—the two primordial Gods, the father and mother of the whole creation! Marduk then becomes the lord of the world, the god of our Earth, and finally the chief god of Babylon. This gives us the impression that good and evil are being described from the subjectively reversed view of their worshippers—a view that is uncritically adopted by ethnologists and theologians. To the critical reader, however, Enki, Anshar, and Marduk may well appear as the real culprits. Are they the thugs of the divine world, who take power over part of Apsu's realm through cunningness and murder?

Later the Anunnaki came to the Earth and "created" human beings here—not out of the primordial energy, which would have been a real creation; rather they manufactured them through genetic manipulation of existing forms of life. (Here as elsewhere, I sometimes place the word *create* in quotation marks, because true creation manifests something out of the primordial energy that was not there before. Making something through manipulation of existing forms is thus not a real creation in the same sense.) The two main gods that took possession of our planet were Enlil and Enki.

Thus the Mesopotamian religion is not, strictly speaking,

polytheistic, since only one is mentioned as a primordial Creator, even though it has two aspects, both male (Apsu) and female (Tiamat); it is in a way androgynous. The other gods are subordinate intermediate beings between the true divine and us humans. Analogously, we could regard Christianity, with its assemblage of God the Father, Christ, the Holy Spirit, Mary, and a large number of angels as at least semipolytheistic—especially if we take into account the veneration of saints. Ethnologists and linguists have given hard evidence that the Bible (particularly Genesis and some other parts of the Pentateuch) essentially has its origin in Mesopotamian texts that were modified and abbreviated. The Bible begins with briefly mentioning the creation of heaven and Earth—the significance of the first sentence in Genesis and the waters mentioned will be discussed later in this book in a different sense (see page 39 regarding *tehom*)—and then the creation of humans. The *Enuma Elish* begins earlier, with the original creation in more detail, and therefore has a section that is missing in the Bible. Theologians and rabbis who resist seeing it this way are merely using tactics to protect their positions.

Anton Parks has written an interesting book, *Eden: The Truth about Our Origins,* in which he translates Mesopotamian texts in a different way from that of many scholars.[3] What is of main interest here is his description of the Anunnaki gods Enki and Enlil.

According to Parks, Enki is Enlil's father, and not, as is otherwise commonly assumed, his brother;[4] Enlil enacted this deception to appear equal to his father. Parks's view deviates from the general view of Enki and Enlil, but it appears to be substantiated by the quotation, "Enlil, may the father who gave you life, Enki, with Ninki [Damkina], say a prayer on my behalf." The translation of this quotation is, however, uncertain.[5] Another text mentions Enlil as the father of Enki.[6] Hence this question has not yet been settled. In any case, Enlil, "the lord of wrath," does not love the human race but despises it. Humans are mere animals to him.

Enki is sometimes described as a snake, perhaps because of his wisdom. The lord of knowledge, he holds the secret of the gods that humans should not know.[7] But transgressing this prohibition, he has revealed certain secrets to the humans. Thus he is friendly to the humans.

THE CELESTIAL CEILING AND THE EARTH

The gods assisting Tiamat tried to escape, but they were caught and their weapons were destroyed. Marduk split the skull of Tiamat and cut her blood vessels. He let the north wind carry her skull (also translated as "her blood") to distant regions, and the gods who were on his side rejoiced. He cut up the rest of the body as a fish is cut up for drying. He let one half of it form a ceiling in the sky. He spread her skin out and assigned a watcher to prevent her "water" (energy) from escaping. From the other part, he formed Esharra—the Earth. He also fashioned abodes for the great gods on Earth.

Marduk set the zodiac in the sky and divided the year in twelve months. He declared Nibiru to be the abode of the gods that announces their duties. Finally he put the Moon in its orbit. This means that he set the orbit of the Earth around the Sun as well as that of the Moon around the Earth. This determines the zodiac and the movement of the Moon, the division of the year into months.

The gods at work here were the Anunnaki, whose highest god was Enki's father Anu, the god of the heavens. Nibiru is regarded by many as their domicile.

THE CREATION
OF HUMANS

Marduk spoke (*Enuma Elish*): "I will form blood and let bones come to be. Then I will make the human being, his name shall be 'man.' Yes, I will make the human! Upon him shall be imposed the duty to serve the gods so that they may rest." Kingu was killed as punishment for provoking Tiamat's fight, and man on Earth was made out of his blood and his bones.

Other clay tablets give more details about how the human race was "created." Another way of "creation" is mentioned, over which the goddess of birth, Ninhursag ("lady of the holy mountains")— also called Mami ("mother"), Nintu ("goddess of birth"), or Belet-Ili ("lady of the gods")—is appointed.

The humans were to cultivate and water the fields so that they would produce much for the Anunnaki. They were also to celebrate the feasts of the gods and keep oxen, sheep, cattle, fish, and poultry. Other tablets mention that the humans were fashioned to serve the gods without freedom of their own.

As slaves of the gods.

A SANCTUARY ON EARTH

Three hundred Anunnaki became watchers of heaven. Another three hundred were assigned for service on Earth. The latter are called *Igigi*. (It is not clear, however, exactly which Anunnaki group is called *Igigi*.)

A high, tower-shaped temple was erected in Babylon, called Esagila, in which lounges for Marduk, Enlil, and Enki were arranged. The Anunnaki also put up altars for themselves. Marduk was, in a quite dictatorial manner, appointed god of the humans by Anu (his grandfather).

WHAT IS NIBIRU?

The *Enuma Elish* mentions Nibiru on tablet 5, line 6 (some translators write *Nebiru* or *Neberu*). Translators into various languages have rendered this by different names—such as *polestar, Jupiter, Mercury, pole of the universe, the one who seizes the middle, the one who seizes Tiamat in the middle, planet of passage* (or crossing)—or it is left untranslated. On tablet 7, lines 124–9, Nibiru is said to be a star that controls the passage between heaven and Earth, and it is the "star of Marduk."

Taken from a number of different translations and versions (into English, German, and French), the following quotations contain about all that the *Enuma Elish* tells us about Nibiru. Material in parentheses consists of variations among these translations (note the remarkably different choices of words):

He established the divisions of the year through signs (constellations of the zodiac; set up three stars each for the twelve months), he established (gave them) the position of Nibiru to determine their relations (mark out their course; fix the distance between the stars). So that no one would go astray (make an omission, an act of negligence; transgress or be slothful), he set up the stations of Enlil and Enki (with Nibiru). He opened gates on both sides and attached strong bolts (locks; a strong corridor) to the left and to the right. He placed the zenith (the heights of heaven; the superior zones) in her (Tiamat's) belly (in her midst; in her liver; in the heavenly vault). (Tablet 5, 3ff.)

He indeed determined the end and the beginning (shall hold the beginning and the future; is the warden of all peoples). As Nibiru, the seizer of the midst (of Tiamat), may he keep the passage (place of crossing) of heaven and the netherworld (between heaven and Earth; keep the turning points of the orbit). They (the gods) should not pass up or down (above or below; everyone who cannot find the passage), but wait for him (pay homage to him). Nibiru is his star that he made to shine in the sky, may it take its position on the heavenly staircase (celestial ladder) so that it can be seen (so that it may maintain beginning and end; so that it may be venerated). Yes, he who constantly (tirelessly; without resting) crosses the sea (forces his way through Tiamat; passes through the middle of Tiamat), his name shall be Nibiru, who controls (grasps; seizes; occupies) her middle (the crossroads). May he uphold the course of the stars of heaven and shepherd all gods like sheep. May he bind (vanquish; subdue) Tiamat and bring mortal danger to her life (constrict her breath; narrow and shorten her life; may her life be straight and short; he conquered Tiamat, he troubled her and ended her life). (Tablet 7, 123ff.)

The translation by Nancy K. Sandars is a bit different, describing Nibiru thus: "He who once crossed the firmament tirelessly now is the nub of the universe."[8] I do not, however, agree with her description of Apsu as "sweet water" or of Tiamat as "bitter water," or with a few other things in her version that she renders according to common academic opinion (cf. footnote on page 4). What here is called *water* is an *energy* (as noted previously), but the narrow worldview of official science cannot conceive of such energies. Therefore it is assumed that Tiamat is the sea or saltwater (not bitter water), while Apsu is the sweet water in the rivers of Mesopotamia. Both are, of course, sustainers of life on Earth. An early and still less plausible translation of Apsu was *abyss*.

It is interesting that Tiamat's life should be described here as short and in mortal danger, since according to the preceding tablets of the *Enuma Elish,* she would already be dead. A translation by Wolfram von Soden (here translated from the German) reads: "Nibiru should hold the passages from heaven to Earth occupied, because everyone above and below who does not find the gateway always asks him. Nibiru is his (Marduk's) star that they made visible in the sky. He takes position at the turning point and then they may look at him and say 'Who without rest crosses the midst of the sea (Tiamat), his name should be Nibiru, because he seizes the midst of it.' They shall keep the path of the stars in the sky unchanged."[9] The remarkable differences in the versions illustrate the difficulties translators have with these passages. The concepts of Tiamat as a "sea" and as an entity are mixed in a rather unclear manner—an uncertainty that to some extent appears to be already present in the original text.

Hardly anyone appears to have taken up the questions: Where would a passage be, and where would the middle of the "sea" (allocated to Tiamat) be? How would a crossing take place here? Is Nibiru watching that passage, and can one cross only with its permission?

Since Nibiru is also called a star or a planet (or in any case a heavenly body), many want to understand it as the domicile of the Anunnaki. Zecharia Sitchin (1920–2010) described it as such in his first book *The 12th Planet*, but there he did not call it Nibiru.[10] He only writes about a "twelfth planet," which he calls "Marduk," because in ancient times, the Moon and the Sun were regarded as planets, and that, along with the nine known to us, makes eleven. If there were one more, it would be the twelfth. In later books such as *The Wars of Gods and Men*[11] and others, he names this hypothetical planet as Nibiru. Sitchin's interpretation of Mesopotamian texts has always been criticized by official science. How can we form an opinion about this matter?

For over a hundred years, official astronomy has speculated that there could be a planet beyond Neptune, called *planet X*, which could explain certain anomalies in the orbits of the known outer planets.[12] There are also speculations about a star, Nemesis (of the brown-dwarf type), which revolves around the Sun far outside the orbits of the known planets and which would have planets of its own.[13] Another outlying speculative planet is Tyche.[14] Still another one is Hercolubus;[15] if it exists, its gravitation would have caused natural catastrophes in ancient times when it came close to Earth. Other names for such a hypothetical planet are "The Destroyer" or "Wormwood" (after a star of that name in Revelation 8:11). A small trans-Neptunian planet, Eris (earlier called Xena), was discovered in 2005 and has a moon named Dysnomia.

Within the frame of such considerations, Sitchin's hypothesis would not be too odd if it were not for the fact that he believed that his twelfth planet was populated—by Anunnaki. Such an opinion is taboo in the scientific world. One carefully refrains from making oneself a subject of colleagues' ridicule or becoming a target for intrigue, because that could mean the end of a career. For mainstream science, extraterrestrials are not allowed to exist, much less alien civilizations, and least of all ones that are ahead of us technologically.

According to Sitchin, the orbit of Nibiru is a long ellipse, like that of a comet. The period of revolution around the Sun would be 3,600 years. In prehistoric times, the planet would have entered our solar system from somewhere in space and then stayed here. The latter fits in with one description of Nibiru in an alternative translation mentioned above: "He who once crossed the firmament tirelessly now is the nub of the universe."

Enuma Elish describes Nibiru as "shining." Hebrew is related to some of the Mesopotamian languages. In Gesenius's Hebrew lexicon, the word *niberash* = "shine, radiate" is mentioned as an unused root.[16] A word that has much the same meaning is *heylal* =

"the shining one" or "the bringer of light," a word that in the Latin translation of the Bible becomes "Lucifer." (A chain of associations that could lead to speculations. . . .)

Parks rightly criticizes Sitchin's hypothesis, since the latter never (or only rarely) supported it with references to sources—beyond the meager information in the *Enuma Elish*—and never answered questions about it.

In my view, Sitchin held back important information in the *Enuma Elish*, such as the deicides—the assassination of Apsu and Tiamat by their own creations. If we take the *Enuma Elish* reasonably seriously (as we are attempting to do here), this scandalous information is extremely important, because it has to do with the apostasy of a corresponding part of the creation, a literal fall of the angels and an original sin, the *sin of sundering,* as it were. Sitchin never mentioned this.

Sitchin's theory about Nibiru has led to a flood of internet posts. Hardly a week passes by when someone does not report having seen Nibiru looking like a second sun or some other apparition in the sky. Videos and pictures have been posted, but it is likely that at least some have been graphically manipulated. I have myself never had such a sighting, and, lacking personal confirmation, I regard this evidence as doubtful. There are also calculations reckoning the orbit and position of Nibiru in the sky as well as the time of its next approach to Earth. They differ considerably and cannot be harmonized. This certainly does not mean that there is no such planet, but it does mean that many are taking us for a ride, constructing their own "reports." Or perhaps it is a matter of disinformation.

At one time I gave more credence to Sitchin's theories than I do today (although even then I did not agree with everything he wrote). They could, however, enable us to understand certain Bible passages in another way than that of conventional dogma.

Some of these will be discussed below. In short, I consider some of his theories to be noteworthy, although they are best taken with a pinch of salt.

There is in my view no real contradiction in interpreting the *Enuma Elish* and other Mesopotamian texts as saying that extraterrestrials have influenced humanity, however taboo such a view may be in the scientific camp. Such an interpretation is not confronted with logical contradictions; instead it is greeted with emotional reactions.

In Parks's opinion, the abode of the gods is not Nibiru but Duku, the holy hill—but only after they arrived on the Earth. Where did they then come from—from a celestial Duku? Marduk(u) could mean either *protector* or *son of Duku*. A mountain in Kharsag or Hursag (possibly an unidentified mountain range or strip of raised land outside the Mesopotamian plain) is also called Duku—the town Kharsag is regarded by some as the prototype of the garden of Eden. On the other hand, *kharsag* in Sumerian means *mountain* in general; it is not the name of a specific mountain. The oldest religious text of Mesopotamia is said to come from there, written on a cylinder that is called the Barton cylinder after its discoverer: George Anton Barton published the first translation of it in 1918.[17]

Parks translates the first section of this text in an interpretive manner: "They came in strength from beyond time, they were carried, one day, by the rebellion [word uncertain] of the universe. Enlil's food would give them life. On behalf of the Lady Serpent (Sir, Ninmah, Ninkharsag) there was an imploration, because she granted the favor that would make all of them live."[18] Barton, by contrast, translated this passage thus: "He came forth, from Kesh he came, Enlil, the food of Enlil gives him life. Unto Sir there is a cry, she grants favor, makes all live."[19] It is unclear from what source Parks has all the other words. Kesh was a Sumerian town, but according to Parks, the word originally meant *universe,* or the rest of the world. Parks describes Enlil as *shatam,* a Sumerian word that according to him means "(territorial) administrator." He explains that there is a character in the Sumerian text that can mean either *lul* (liar) or *shatam,* and he chooses the latter. At this point he discusses the identity of Satan and incorrectly asserts a relation to the Hebrew word *satam,* which, he says, means *hate* or *pursue,* although it actually means *stop, prevent,* or *snare.* (I will take this subject up again later.) Enlil is also called "lord (who came) from the night and of our men of well-drilling" and "lord of the storm and our men of the pickax."

Parks's translation here mentions the diseases that have been imposed on humans "from above" to reduce their numbers, because they (probably with the help of Enki) had achieved unauthorized access to the "garden of the gods" (cf. the Flood story on page 23). But Enki took some effort to prepare a remedy in the form of an alcoholic beverage (probably an herbal tincture or a beer made from fermented fruits and herbs).

Reading, with Parks, that the gods came from somewhere "beyond time" because of a "rebellion of the universe" to settle in Duku fits in with Sitchin's theory about Nibiru as a celestial body that came from beyond our solar system; does the statement "Enlil came from the night" refer to the interstellar darkness? Even though there is room for doubt, this theory does not appear fully out of place. It deserves to be taken into consideration.

It is not at all astonishing that Parks—like Sitchin, but in different ways—has been strongly criticized for his translations and interpretations and has been called a source of disinformation by representatives of the "classical" view.[20] Naturally one side will want to defend this view and will therefore denigrate anyone who does not belong to the club. At the same time much of the criticism of Parks appears justified to me. As usual, the truth is likely to lie in the middle. Readers may try to draw their own conclusions from the references in endnote 20 (even though they are in French). In any case, Parks's translations are remarkably wordy and so interpretive that his translations are often considerably longer than the conventional ones, often containing words that are not found in other translations.

TIAMAT:
THE CELESTIAL CEILING

Sitchin considers the celestial ceiling to be the asteroid belt. How did this belt come to be? There is an empirical rule in astronomy called the Titius-Bode law. It is expressed through the formula $R_n = 4 + 3 \cdot 2^n$, where R_n is a measure for the mean radius of a planetary orbit and n is the number of the planet, counting from the Sun but beginning with Venus. For Venus, then, $n = 0$, for the Earth $n = 1$, and so on. For $n = 3$, however, there is a gap between Mars and Jupiter. Here one would expect to find a planet, but instead there is a gigantic number of asteroids, rocks, and stones, called the asteroid belt. It has been suggested that these could be remnants of a hypothetical planet that burst asunder, called Mallona or Phaeton. Today's astronomy has alternative explanations and has distanced itself from this theory, but it may nevertheless be of interest, because it is not unlikely.

Sitchin claims that this planet, which he calls Tiamat, had come to a collision course with Nibiru, because the latter would have an elongated elliptic orbit that crosses the orbits of the other planets (which would fit the expression "planet of crossing"). He interprets the mythic fight between Marduk (Nibiru) and Tiamat as a real physical collision, in which the planet Tiamat was crushed to pieces by a moon of Nibiru. About half of Tiamat broke into rubble and debris, which then formed the asteroid belt. The other half was thrown out of the orbit, later to form the Earth (Esharra).

If we hypothetically regard the *Enuma Elish* as more than just a myth and consider Sitchin's claim that Nibiru would have been (and still is) populated by the Anunnaki, we may ask if the planet Tiamat was also populated. In that case, each of the two populations may have attempted to save themselves by diverting the orbit of the other planet or, if necessary, destroying it. It is not clear why Sitchin calls the planet Tiamat, but it could have had a civilization belonging to another region of the creation and not in accord with the "renegade" Anunnaki from the other enclave (see page 6), in some way like two different political camps, of which one was oriented toward Tiamat.

Parks instead claims that Nibiru was a moon of the exploded planet Phaeton (Tiamat). That is hardly consistent with the destruction of the planet. How could it then have burst to pieces? As a result, Sitchin's collision theory seems to fit better.

One thing that representatives of official science will find disagreeable is the claim that the ancient Anunnaki were more advanced technologically than we are today, at least in regard to their mastery of space travel and their ability to manipulate life-forms genetically. How could that be possible? One answer would have to do with the fact that our universe is beyond any doubt *multidimensional*. Present-day physics acknowledges that the cosmos has more than the three dimensions that we Earth humans can perceive with our limited sensory organs. (Was this limitation genetically engineered into us?) If the universe has many more than these three dimensions, it is not far-fetched to think that there may also be *multidimensional life-forms* there. If the Anunnaki were, for example, five-dimensional beings, they would be able to do things we cannot even imagine. That would also explain how they could live on a planet that would be uninhabitable for us three-dimensionals, because it spends very long periods in a cosmic night and cold far from the Sun.

COULD NIBIRU BE OUR MOON?

If we consider the possibility that these gods can travel in space, Nibiru could be viewed as a space station in the "sea of Tiamat" (interplanetary space), which, as a floating border sentry, controls the passage between the Earth and extraterrestrial space. This could be big enough to be visible as a "star." Or could Nibiru be a base on our Moon?

Or is it actually the Moon itself? There is a theory, presented by two Russian scientists, Michael Vasin and Alexander Shcherbakov, in 1978 that the Moon could be a hollowed-out planetoid that functions as a huge spaceship.[21] This could explain some strange properties of this satellite. Such a hypothesis would fit in quite well with the description in the *Enuma Elish*.

Both, of course, could be true: there could be an Anunnakian presence on (or in) the Moon *as well as* on a planet X. There is increasing evidence today that there may really be such a planet, even though it is not easy to separate the chaff from the wheat as far as the evidence is concerned. Nevertheless, the description of Nibiru in the *Enuma Elish* would apply better to the Moon. The hypothesis of a planet X does not fit in very well with the sparse information given in the *Enuma Elish*. But perhaps planet X is simply not mentioned in that text.

The text talks about passing through the "sea" (Tiamat) and through her "middle." The "sea" could be the space in our solar system, while the "middle of Tiamat" makes us think of the asteroid belt, which was formed in the midst of our planetary system from a planet associated with Tiamat. Is the passage through this region, through the "middle of Tiamat," from planet X toward us, or the other way? That could also make us think of Nibiru as the planet Jupiter (Marduk's planet), which in some way could be regarded as a "watcher" in or near that region in space.

Seen from various sides, there are different possibilities, but in my opinion Nibiru and planet X are not identical, although this does not exclude the possibility that the latter also exists. Probably both exist, creating a confusion in identification. In any case, it appears that Sitchin was the first to regard the two as one and the same.

MORE ABOUT THE "CREATION" OF HUMANS

Two kinds of "creation" of humans are described in the Sumerian clay tablets. First, they mention a "sprouting forth" of humans like plants out of the earth, which took place at a specific location called Uzumúa ("where flesh is made to grow").[22] These were a kind of humanoid animal rather than real humans. They did not know to eat bread or how to wear clothes, and they walked on their hands and feet and ate grass like sheep. Another myth says that at that location humans were made to "sprout forth" out of the blood of slaughtered gods, which may link the two kinds of creation to each other. In this way the humans emerged from an animalistic state. They were given the breath of life (which may mean souls), and thus became real humans, who practiced farming.

The *second* kind of "creation," which Sitchin holds to be a *genetic intervention* by the gods, is explained in more detail below.

The text *Atra-Hasis* mentions that the group of gods called the Igigi had to work hard.[23] After forty years, they rebelled and burned their tools. Then they went to Enlil and troubled him with threats of war. The work they were ordered to do was too hard, and now they wanted to settle with Enlil. Enki suggested that humans should be "manufactured" to bear the yoke. A goddess of birth, Belet-Ili (also called Mami, Nintu, or Ninmah; see page 10), was to carry out this task. The gods mixed clay with blood and the flesh of a slaughtered god. Fourteen chosen goddesses were to carry this mixture to term. The children, seven of whom had male and seven female dispositions, were born after ten months. They became the first workers, and they were called *lullu*. From then on, they were to multiply through a physical union between man and woman. These humans, made to be slaves, had black hair on their heads; therefore they were also called the "blackheads."

What is the "clay" that is mentioned here? The gods took it from "above in *abzu*."[24] Here *abzu* may refer to Enki's temple, in which there was "holy water" (special energies?). [25] The "clay" would then probably be a substrate for a kind of genetic process. Blood and flesh contain genes, even when they come from an Anunnaku. (Since the word *Anunnaki* designates a people of gods, it is inherently plural, and I will use *Anunnaku* as a simplified singular.)

The process was not immediately successful, however, because in the beginning some of the humans had defects, according to the text *Enki and Ninmah*.[26] In preliminary trials, a man resulted that could not use his arms; there was another who could not close his eyes; still another with paralyzed feet; an incontinent man; a sterile woman; and a sexless creature. The birth goddess was disappointed. Enki then intervened and recommended pouring the ejaculate of a man into the womb of a woman. Again this produced an incapacitated human. What happened next is written on around ten lines missing from the tablet. But in the end, the gods finally had their human workers.

What then was the work of the Igigi and later the humans? The *Atra-Hasis* tells us that they were digging irrigation canals, such as the rivers Euphrates and Tigris, as well as canals and sources for water. The earth they dug out was heaped up into mountains. Sitchin claims that they were also digging for gold so that they could spread gold dust in the atmosphere of their own planet to reduce the escape of heat, rather like a thermos-bottle effect. (According to Sitchin, Nibiru cools down during the millennia it spends far away from the Sun.) He also suggests that gold was an elixir of life for the gods, even though it did not have the same value as it has for us in terms of wealth (or humans may have come to regard it as valuable because of demand from the Anunnaki).

In his book *Slave Species of the Gods,* Michael Tellinger also says that the main interest of the Anunnaki was to take precious metals, especially gold, from our planet. [27] In my opinion, however, he refers a bit too uncritically to Sitchin's theories, which he supplements with his own research (he takes Sitchin's fictional text *The Lost Book of Enki* remarkably seriously). He found a whole series of ruins in South Africa that, he claims, could have been settlements of the Anunnaki and where gold was probably mined.[28] In Zimbabwe there are enigmatic ruins and gold mines of prehistoric origin.[29]

THE FLOOD

Atra-Hasis, the Akkadian myth of the Flood, reports an evil deed of Enlil towards the humans. He did not like them: they had become "too many and too loud" for him. He ordered diseases and drought to be inflicted upon them in order to reduce their numbers. But this was not enough for him, and he planned a deluge to eradicate them. He forbade Enki to warn the humans about this, but Enki transgressed his command with a trick.

Enki spoke to a wall of reed so that Atra-Hasis could hear

him: "Flee the house, build a boat, forsake possessions, and save life." Enki described how the boat should be built. Atra-Hasis spoke to the assembly of the elders: "My god does not agree with your god, Enki and Enlil are constantly angry with each other. They have expelled me from the land. Since I have always reverenced Enki, I cannot live in your town. Nor can I set my feet on the earth of Enlil."

The ship was built. Various animals (apparently "slaughtered"— their DNA kept, as in a genetic bank?) and Atra-Hasis's family were brought on board. His heart was broken, and he vomited bile. The weather changed, and the storm god Adad began to roar in the clouds. Atra-Hasis sealed the door with pitch and loosed anchor. An enormous deluge came. It became completely dark, and the Sun could no longer be seen. People could not recognize one another in the catastrophe. After seven days, it was possible to go ashore again, and Atra-Hasis offered a sacrifice to the gods.

The gods were hungry, because there were no more farmers and no offerings were being brought. The great mother goddess lamented bitterly about Enlil's and Anu's incompetent decisions and the masses of dead bodies in the rivers. Enki admitted to having helped the humans to survive and convinced Enlil to adopt a better plan.

When they heard that Atra-Hasis had escaped, Enki and Nintu made a plan to ensure that the noise of the people would stay within limits. Death was required. To keep population growth low, children were to die, and taboos of celibacy were issued. A female demon, Pasittu, was to take away children from the laps of women who had given birth. (Pasittu seems also to have been called Lamashtu and resembles Lilith in Hebrew mythology, who kills newborn children; see page 53). The birth canal was narrowed, so that a third of the women would not give birth successfully. Many women would have to live a monastic life.[30]

In a similar but shorter Flood myth, Atra-Hasis is called Ziusudra. The famous *Gilgamesh* epic tells a similar story, and there his name is Utnapishtim. This text relates another story about Enlil's evil. He had "created" a giant, Humbaba, who ruled over a large cedar forest and was involved in the wickedness of the people in the land. To free the people from this evil influence, the hero Gilgamesh, together with his friend Enkidu, killed the giant. Even though Enlil himself had schemed to provoke the fight (probably hoping that Gilgamesh would be killed), Enlil decreed that, as punishment, one of the two friends should die. Enkidu became sick and died, and Gilgamesh grieved heavily.[31]

The epic also tells about Enlil's wrath when he heard that humans had survived the deluge: "Has any of these mortals escaped? Not one was to have survived the destruction." Enki then said to him, "Wisest of gods, hero Enlil, how could you so senselessly bring down the flood?"

THE SUMERIAN TREE OF KNOWLEDGE

In his translations from the Sumerian, Parks interprets the "tree of knowledge" and its fruits as referring to certain tools, because the Sumerian word *gish,* "tree," can also mean "tool."[32] A tool such as a knife or an ax has a wooden handle, like the branch of a tree; the head, a piece of metal, would then be the "fruit." This is allegedly a pun between two very similar Sumerian words *búru* (tool; plundering) and *buru* (fruit of a tree).

In Parks's view, Enki taught humans about a "chisel," which made the gods nervous, because such a tool can also be used as a weapon. The gods also complained that through Enki humans were enjoying their fate and developed a taste for "luxury."[33] Because their fate would improve each time Enki taught them something new, imparting the use of metals to them was regarded as the highest treason. Other translations by Parks, in his view, support the idea that metallurgy in the hands of humans was of major concern to the gods.

But the association of a tree and its fruit with metallic tools certainly appears far-fetched.

In my view, the gods' concern would have a much wider context than merely the use of a knife or an ax, especially in relation to the tree of knowledge (according to Parks, the "tree of penetration"). Comparisons with other translations of relevant texts indicate that the translation "metal" is not without alternatives.[34] No other translation of the texts would support this interpretation. They all differ remarkably from Parks's version, and the word "metal" is found in none of them. Since to my mind there is a lack of logic in Parks's understanding, I consider it a mistake to regard the "secret of the gods" as knowledge about metallurgy.

As an example, Parks's translation of the Sumerian tablet CBS 8322, published by Barton, results in a completely different understanding. Parks's version is, again, very wordy and contains many words that are found nowhere in Barton's edition. Even though Barton calls this text "enigmatic," there is no reason to understand it the way Parks does.[35] Here the text is not as enigmatic as it becomes in Parks's interpretation.

THE TREE OF WISDOM

Parks's book *Eden* contains a remarkable error on page 181, where he claims that the "tree of knowledge" in the Bible would be called *'etz yada'* (page 191 in the French text; in both spelled *Éts Iada*), whereas in the Hebrew text in Genesis it is called *'etz ha-da'at.*

The real meaning of this is *Tree of Wisdom*. The verb *yada'* ("to know") would actually fit his alternative interpretation of the Sumerian text as a "tree of penetration," which he associates with a "penetrating tool" like a knife. The verb *yada'* has two meanings: (1) to know and (2) to have sexual union with (penetration). See Genesis 4:1: "And Adam knew Eve his wife; and she conceived, and bare Cain." But the word *da'at* (knowledge) is not used here! There is no *'etz yada'* in the Bible. *Da'at* does not have an alternative meaning of sexual union or any other kind of "penetration" (except, maybe, to "penetrate" forbidden knowledge). Since ancient times, it has been politically useful to contend that this tree has something to do with sexuality, but *da'at* simply does not have such an alternative meaning. Consequently, the biblical context can only mean that Yahweh forbade seeking knowledge. Humans were not to know too much, especially not about certain secrets. On other non-Sumerian clay tablets it may actually look a bit different, since a few texts indicate that Enki did teach Adam and Eve how to reproduce—but no prohibition was involved. Nor is there any connection with a tree. This subject will be taken up again below.

Here it may be relevant that Enki is also called "god of wisdom." Is all this actually about a prohibition from dealing with him?

WHAT DO THE ANUNNAKI LOOK LIKE?

A widespread opinion holds that the Anunnaki are reptilian entities. A large number of images and sculptures from Mesopotamia (as well as from ancient Egypt) show humanoid figures with animal heads, some of which could, with a bit of imagining, be held to be reptilian.[36] Some figures are shown having wings. An image from the museum in Baghdad could, for example, be showing a figure with scales.[37] (This is admittedly speculative.) A group of gods, the four Apkallu, are described as amphibious beings with bodies like fish.[38] In the third century BCE, the Babylonian Berossos wrote a history of the Babylonians in Greek, in which he mentions the god Oannes, who had the body of a fish, with human legs and feet. He taught many things to humans.[39]

The question about the age these beings could live to creates a puzzling archaeological problem, and quite a headache for eth-nologists.[40] There is a tablet with a list of the Sumerian kings that states their ruling periods using the time unit shar.[41] The first king in the list, Alulim, ruled 8 shars (or sharshar).* A shar is alleg-edly equal to 3,600 years, so that king would have ruled 28,800 years! The longest rule given is for En-men-lu-ana—12 shars or 43,200 years! That cannot be. It appears that equating a shar with 3,600 years goes back to Berossos, who indiscriminately handed down this information from much older sources unknown to us.[42] The meaning of shar is in any case controversial among experts. In cuneiform writing, the word "shar" is in this context (it is dif-ferent in other contexts) represented by a solid circle ● (possibly also with an empty circle ○), signifying a *revolution* or cycle (but also world, ball, entirety). Is this the length of Nibiru's orbit? That is how Sitchin and others see it. A shar cannot be an Earth year, however, since then all these kings would have ruled for short peri-ods only. Therefore we must leave it as undecided what revolution may mean here. Jupiter is regarded as Marduk's planet and has a revolution period of 12 years. Could this be the shar? Then the ruling time of Alulim would be 96 years, which is much more plausible. It has also been suggested that a shar would be

---

*In Sumerian, plurals for things and concepts are indicated through doubling (*sharshar* for shar). Here I use the English plural ending *shars,* as is common in international literature.

The Semitic fish-god Dagon. He is unlike the typical Anunnaku, but he bears a resemblance to Oannes. Illustration from *Illustrerad verldshistoria utgifven av E. Wallis* [Illustrated world history, published by. E. Wallis], volume I. Stockholm: Central-Tryckeriets Förlag, 1875.

3,600 days, that is, slightly less than 10 years. This appears to be a speculative oversimplification, even though it does result in plausible time periods.

Another possibility is indicated in *Suda* (also known as *Suidas*), an anonymous Greek encyclopedia from the tenth century CE. For the Chaldeans, a *shar* was a period of 222 Moon months, amounting to 18.5 years.[43] A Moon month (synodic month) is the time between two full moons (or new moons), and 223 Moon months is said to be the time between two Moon eclipses (there are somewhat different concepts and definitions, such as a related but similar saros cycle, but we need not go into all the rather complicated details and theories of Chaldean and Babylonian astronomy here). Such a cycle could possibly fit in with the idea that Nibiru could be our Moon (see page 20). This too would result in plausible lengths of reign. (In a mathematically amateurish manner, Harrison calculates in a peculiar way and rather arrives back at the original values in shars but with a new interpretation.)[44]

A shar is, however, not only a measure of time but is also used in other contexts with varying numerical values.* Only as a *pure number* is a shar $60^2 = 3,600$. As a measure of time, the word could therefore have another meaning, but here its meaning as a pure number has been arbitrarily applied to its value as a time unit. The concept *cycle* might hypothetically fit the cuneiform character for shar, but then the question remains about what cycle this would be referring to. I find the hypothesis of Moon months plausible.

---

*In surface geometry, a *s(h)ar* can be 12 × 12 *kush*, or around 36 square meters, as well as 6 *buru* = 388.8 hectares. In solid geometry, it is one surface-shar times 1 (Sumerian) yard, or around 18 cubic meters. As a measure in building technology, it is 1,200 brick stones. See A. O. Nissen et al., *Archaic Bookkeeping* (Chicago: University of Chicago Press, 1993), 28–9, and *Reallexikon der Assyriologie* (Berlin: Walter de Gruyter, 1987–90), 7:457–517.

Also related to this question is the fact that the Mesopotamian cultures had a numerical system based on 60. Our system is based on 2 × 5 = 10, because we have five fingers on two hands. The Mesopotamians also counted on their fingers,[45] but that becomes a bit complicated with five fingers. It would be easier with six fingers: a system based on 60 would quite naturally result. Do the Anunnaki have six fingers? The Bible mentions a giant with six fingers (2 Samuel 21:20). Interestingly, today there are still persons on our Earth who, from a genetic predisposition, have six fingers or six toes, or both.[46] A speculative question: because of genetic remnants from the Anunnaki?

These kings may not, however, have been Anunnaki but rather may have been installed by them. Some esoteric sources claim that an Anunnaku could live 1,000 years and, with special life-prolonging measures (probably only for the elite), up to 10,000 years. If that is so, Enki and Enlil may still be around somewhere in their multidimensional bodies. In any case, they will still be present as entities (like the human soul after the death of the body).

HOW DO THE ANUNNAKI FEED THEMSELVES?

As has already been mentioned, there is no doubt that the universe is multidimensional, and we may assume that the Anunnaki are so as well. Since we Earth humans live in this multidimensional universe, we too are multidimensional, but we do not know it, because our organs of perception are impaired so that we perceive only three dimensions. The Anunnaki's are not. Hence they have conscious access to energies of other dimensions that are hidden to us, and they can feed on them. When they are on the Earth, there are also other possibilities for them.

When an Earth human dies and the soul leaves the body, the life energies in the corpse are also set free. These energies can be perceived by an entity with a multidimensional consciousness, whether it is incarnated in a three-dimensional body or not, and it can feed on them as well. This is easier when a human being dies from violence, since the body is still "fully charged." When a person dies from old age or disease in an ailing body, there is almost no life energy left; his batteries are empty, so to speak. This is of no interest to vampiric entities. Furthermore, humans release similar energies when they have very strong negative emotions, especially intense rage, fear, panic, or hatred. Entities and other multidimensional beings can also feed on such energies, as well as on sexual feelings that have to do with lust but not love. Just as a plant can feed on our physical excrement, they can feed on our emotional excrement.[47]

Positive entities feed directly on the primordial divine light energy of the original Creator, which is the primordial source of all nutrition. Those, however, who have cut themselves off from the original Creator, like the Anunnaki, cannot do that but feed indirectly, from the life energies of other living beings, which have better access to the energy of light. We humans have such access, because we feed on plants (vegetables and fruits) that absorb light energy from the Sun and combine it with substances taken from the Earth to produce nutrients. Or we feed on animals that have absorbed light energy from eating plants. (It is still more indirect if we feed on carnivorous animals that have themselves fed on other animals—have you ever wondered why we are not supposed to eat meat from carnivorous animals?) Vampiric entities similarly absorb light energy indirectly, by way of our life energies.

It is therefore no wonder that beings like the Anunnaki like to see violence among us humans. They stir up murder and manslaughter wherever they can and thus get access to the life energies that have been released. To them we are like breeding cattle (in biblical terms, *goyim*). That also explains the purpose of animal sacrifice and still more of human sacrifice. The gods do not take any satisfaction from carcasses, but from the life energies that come out of a body with its shed blood, because "blood is a fluid with curious properties" (as Goethe said in *Faust*, part 1, line 1740) and is a carrier of life energies. This also offers them a way to the above-mentioned life-prolonging measures. If the victim suffers in the process, so much the better, because then emotional energies are also set free.

The epic *Gilgamesh* relates that at the end of the flood Utnapishtim brought a sacrifice to the gods, and "the gods smelled the sweet odor of the sacrificial animal and gathered like flies over the sacrifice." A scene that tells more than the mere words. . . .

This explains the prohibition against eating blood. Humans are forbidden from consuming blood (Leviticus 3:17; 7:27). Instead animals are to be ritually killed by cutting their throats and letting the blood flow out (*shechita*) before eating the meat.[48] The blood is for the gods and the meat for the humans.

2

IS YAHWEH ENLIL?

Biblical Origins in the Cuneiform Texts of Mesopotamia

The Mesopotamian Flood stories remind us to such an extent of the one in the Bible that there must be a connection. But there are many other correspondences as well.

Here I will first discuss the very beginning of the Bible.

THE FIRST SENTENCE IN THE BIBLE

The Hebrew text in Gen 1:1 reads as follows: *Bere'shit bara' 'elohim et ha-shamayim ve'et ha'aretz,* usually translated as: "In the beginning God created the heaven and the Earth."

However you twist and turn it, it remains a fact that that *'elohim* is the plural of *'eloah = god.* It has therefore been suggested that it be understood as "the gods created . . . " but this does not fit grammatically, because the verb *bara'* (*created*) has the singular form. Theologians then sweep this under the carpet and declare it to be a *pluralis maiestatis* (the plural of majesty or the "royal we"). This grammatical form does exist in Hebrew,[1] but there is another solution to the problem that is probably overlooked on purpose.

The conventional and dogmatically approved translation of *bere'shit* is based on the translation of *be* as *in* or *at* and *reshit* as *beginning*. According to dictionaries, *re'shit* can alternatively mean the first of its kind, and *be* can refer to the origin. Thus the word *bere'shit* can also be seen as a somewhat tautological expression meaning "the original first" or "the very first" or "the primordial Creator." Then the following fits grammatically:

The First One created the gods, the heavens, and the Earth, or, a bit more freely: *The primordial Creator created the gods, the cosmic worlds, and the Earth.*

Furthermore, very few translations have "the heavens," keeping the plural of the original text, since the Hebrew word *shamayim*, "heaven," also has the plural form and can meaningfully be understood as "cosmic worlds." Who, then, are the created gods? In our context, obviously the inhabitants of other cosmic worlds—planets and other-dimensional realms—that is, *extraterrestrial life in general*: the Anunnaki and the other gods out there. As mentioned above, if we can hypothetically view the Mesopotamian texts as being based on facts, this could mean that the Anunnaki have annexed one region of the creation, in which case there will also have to be other regions.

This interpretation has some support in the light of otherwise enigmatic plurals in the Bible (emphasis added): "And God said, Let *us* make man in *our* image, after *our* likeness" (Genesis 1:26).

"And the LORD God said, Behold, the man is become as one of *us,* to know good and evil" (Genesis 2:22).

In both quotes, the Hebrew text has *'Elohim,* in the latter quote even *Yahweh* (the LORD) *'Elohim.* I will discuss the latter combination further starting on page 40. This designation of the biblical god is found rather often, and it gives further support for this interpretation.

Many passages in the Bible mention "gods": "Who is like unto thee, O LORD, among the *gods*?" (Exodus 15:11). "Thou shalt make no covenant with them, nor with their *gods* . . . for if thou serve their *gods*, it will surely be a snare unto thee" (Exodus 23:32–3; emphasis added here and in the following quotes). "Upon their *gods* also the LORD executed judgments" (Numbers 33:4—how could he do that if they do not exist?), and many other passages. The Lord was furious about Gentiles sacrificing their children—"for even their sons and their daughters they have burnt in the fire to their *gods*" (Deuteronomy 12:31)—and what does he do then? "When the Lord thy God shall have *destroyed* before thy face the nations, which thou then shalt go in to *possess*, and when thou shalt *possess* them, and dwell in their land" (Deuteronomy 12:29), he himself sends his hosts to kill them and their children. (I have taken the translation "destroyed" from the Douay-Rheims Bible. Other versions usually translate *yakrit* as "cut off," from the verb *karat*, which also means *kill, destroy,* and *cut down,* like a tree—in this case obviously with swords.)

THE MESOPOTAMIAN
FLOOD STORIES AND THE BIBLE

Even in the beginning of the translation and study of the Mesopotamian texts, the remarkable correspondences between these stories and the ones in the Bible aroused the attention of ethnologists and linguists, especially concerning the Flood. As early as 1876, a publication about this subject appeared by George Smith: *The Chaldean Account of Genesis*.[2] A little later, a study was issued in the classic work *Die Keilinschriften und das alte Testament*

(The cuneiform inscriptions and the Old Testament) by Eberhard Schrader,[3] with a contribution by Paul Haupt.[4] Another classic treatment of this subject is the contribution by Heinrich Zimmern in the book *Schöpfung und Chaos in Urzeit und Endzeit* (Creation and chaos in primeval times and in the end times) by Hermann Gunkel.[5] A newer work about this was written by Alexander Heidel: *The Gilgamesh Epic and the Old Testament Parallels.*[6] The reactions to such publications were divided, as could be expected. For devout Christians and Jews, it was impossible that there could be a divine revelation earlier than the Bible. Theologians and rabbis tried by any means to disprove a connection. For them, there could only be three explanations:

1. The similarities are coincidental.
2. The Mesopotamian stories are copied from or inspired by those in the Bible.
3. They are independent stories about real incidents.

It was easier for agnostics and atheists: the stories are mere fairytales. Scholars tried to devalue the correspondences by pointing out various differences between the stories, but the many similarities remain striking. Furthermore, the *Enuma Elish* contains a prehistory about the creation of the Earth and of life on our planet that is merely hinted at in the Bible.

The differences are actually comparatively minor. In the clay tablets, the Flood was sent upon the Earth because the gods wanted to have peace and rest from the humans, who had become annoying to them; in the Bible, it was because the humans had become sinful. In the tablets, Enki warns Atra-Hasis secretly. In the Bible, god warns Noah directly. The shape of the ark is different in the stories. In the tablet texts, it rained seven days, in the Bible text forty days. In the Bible, Noah was told to repopulate the

Earth; in the tablets a group of people escaped with Atra-Hasis, and then the Earth could be repopulated. In both stories, birds are sent out to find land. In the Bible, a raven returns, and then a dove comes back with an olive twig. In the Mesopotamian story, a dove and a swallow return, but not the raven. There are a few more such details.

An extensive discussion of these parallels was published in 1997 in the magazine *Bible and Spade*.[7] This magazine is issued by an organization that holds the Bible to be infallible, so the discussion proceeds according to that view. It reveals how many of the arguments used to contradict the correspondence theory are forced (some may believe that the quantity of arguments is more important than their quality). Such difficulties aside, the discussion gives a good overview of the similarities.

FURTHER CORRESPONDENCES

Besides the Flood story, there are many other correspondences between the Bible and the Mesopotamian texts, not least between the *Enuma Elish* and the biblical creation story in Genesis. Both are based on the concept of a primordial energy, which is an *entity* that out of itself created worlds and living beings. This original energy existed in an original chaos, surrounded by darkness. But what is chaos? The word is usually understood as meaning complete disorder, but the original meaning is "total emptiness." It is derived from the Greek word *khaino*, which means "yawn"—as in the expression "the yawning void"—and it corresponds to *tohu va-bohu* in Genesis 1:2, which means "waste and void." The primordial chaos was simply pure energy that so far was without content, because no creation either in or outside of it had taken place. In both stories, light emanated from the Creator God—in the Mesopotamian story in the form that this primordial energy *is* light—and he made worlds come to be. The gods later "created" humans similar to themselves out of "clay" or "dust." At the end, in the *Enuma Elish* the gods celebrated; in the Bible God rests.

It has also been claimed that the Hebrew word *tehom* ("depth," but also "body of water," "sea") in Genesis 1:2 is etymologically related to Tiamat (which, however, has been tendentiously questioned on linguistic grounds).[8] Heidel regards the two words as having the same origin but asserts that they have different meanings.[9]

A certain correspondence can also be found in the *twofold* creation of humans. As mentioned on page 21, there are two different stories about their creation in the Mesopotamian texts. The Bible has certain parallels to this also. The first creation of humans is described in Genesis 1:26–7: "And God said, Let *us* make man in *our* image. . . . So God created man in his own image, in the image of God created he him; male and female created he them" (emphasis added). The word here translated as *God* is, again, *'Elohim*, actually "the gods." That took place on the sixth day in the biblical story, hence man and woman were created simultaneously and as equals. Then followed a second creation of humans in Genesis 2:7, 2:22.

Enki had a book with the *me*, more than one hundred divine laws and commandments (also described as divine powers).[10] These were written on clay tablets, of which today only fragments exist. It has been suggested that they could be compared to the tablets with the commandments given to Moses. The god of these commandments was Enmesharra (a god of the underworld, an ancestor of Enki and Enlil who is not mentioned in the *Enuma Elish*). Enlil gathered them and gave them to Enki.

Adam is not the first man. He is created only after the seventh day and apparently in another way. He comes onstage in the second chapter of Genesis. "And there was not a man to till the ground" (Genesis 2:5; but maybe there was already a man somewhere else, outside Eden, with other or no tasks). Therefore god* created Adam out of the dust of the ground and breathed the breath of life into his nostrils (Genesis 2:7). Here nothing is said about his being made in the likeness of god (but see Genesis 5:1). Adam was put in the Garden of Eden, in a way as god's gardener. His name in the first place means *man*, but it can be related to other meanings as well. He is alone until a woman is created for him quite some time later.

Here the Hebrew word translated as "dust" is *'aphar*. It means something that is pulverized or ground to dust, or particles. "Earth" as dust ("of the ground") is *'adamah*. This is explained by the premise that the earth of the Orient is usually reddish, and *'adam* can also mean "red," "reddish," "the color of blood." A somewhat far-fetched explanation. But the Hebrew word *dam* means "blood." Could we also understand "dust of the earth" as red blood cells? After all, it would be far-fetched to assume that the raw material for Adam would be dry dust gathered from the ground. If we were to understand this material as the components of blood, we would come close to the Mesopotamian creation story (created out of the blood of a slaughtered god!). Blood cells carry genes, and with that we come close to Sitchin's theories about a genetic process. "Dust of *the earth*" could specifically refer to blood cells of *terrestrial* origin, maybe from animals or some kind of pre-historic humans, which were then mixed with genes of the gods.

Here god is not called *'Elohim* but *Yahweh 'Elohim*, so that he appears to be one of the 'elohim (created gods) who makes his own "creation."

Adam and Eve ate from the tree of knowledge and had to leave Eden. They soon had children, and their son Cain took himself

---

*Here "god" is written with a lowercase "g," for reasons that will be explained on page 46, since he is the one we call Yahweh and can identify with Enlil.

a wife (Genesis 4:17). His sons also took wives. Where did they come from? The solution to the riddle can only be that god or the gods had "created" other humans before Adam and they could actively reproduce (Genesis 1:28). That explains Cain's otherwise puzzling fear that anyone who would find him could kill him for his brother's murder (Genesis 4:14). According to the common dogmatic interpretation, there would be no others who could do it. His parents, his wife, and his children would probably not—at most, then, perhaps the gods.

The Mesopotamian literature contains a story about Adapa, who, because of an unfortunate incident, was called to the abode of Anu for questioning.[11] At the end of the conversation, Anu sends Adapa back: "Take him back to his Earth!" Hence Anu's abode is not on our planet. It has repeatedly been suggested that this is a parallel to the biblical story about Adam in Eden, but I do not find this very convincing. But something else strikes me. At the entrance to Anu's abode, there are two "watchers," Tammuz and Gishzida. Tammuz (Dumuzi, Du'zu) is the Sumerian god of food, vegetation, and farming, while Gishzida (Gizzida, Ningishzida) is the lord of the "good tree" and of healing. These remind us of the two trees in the Garden of Eden. One may also speculate about parallels to the two pillars, Jachin and Boaz, at the entrance to Solomon's temple (1 Kings 7:21).

Further correspondences have been studied extensively in the literature.[12] An interesting overview by the well-known Assyriologist Wilfred George Lambert (1926–2011)[13] is published in the renowned German encyclopedia *Theologische Realenzyklopädie*,[14] in which he visibly strives to play down the significance of the many correspondences, even though the unbiased reader will regard them as important evidence. I suppose he did so because he was a Christadelphian[15] and thus belonged to a community that strives to live their lives and faith exclusively according to the word of god as written in the Bible.[16] Therefore any proof of a Mesopotamian origin of the biblical texts would conflict with his personal beliefs.

It is interesting that some authors give an overview of these correspondences and parallels with the intention of devaluing them, and even so provide helpful material for discussion.

WHO IS YAHWEH?

Yahweh is the god in the Hebrew Bible and in the Old Testament of the Christian Bible. It is in the Bible written only with consonants as YHWH, since in Judaism his name is not to be pronounced. Instead, when referring to him, one is to say *Adonai*. This word is an ancient plural (again!) of *adon* = lord. There are various theories about which vowels could be applied to the four consonants. The name is also called the Tetragrammaton or "the four letters." Today the generally accepted theological pronunciation is "Yahweh," but a common variant is "Yehowah," approximately adopting the vocalization of *Adonai*. He explains his name himself as "I am that I am" in Exodus 3:14.*

---

*A speculation. The word YHWH may be associated with "he is" as follows. We may divide it in YH+HUH, keeping the middle H in both parts and reading the Hebrew letter *vav* as U, a valid alternative that depends on missing diacritical marks. HUH could be derived from HU' that means "he" and if we add an initial H to the first part: HYH, we get a word that according to the Hebrew dictionary means "to be, exist," from which 'HYH (*eh[e]yeh*) is derived. Therefore, we could regard YHWH as a kind of contraction of the words *ehyeh asher ehyeh* in Exodus 3:14. The controversial but very knowledgeable German linguist Friedrich Delitzsch (1850–1922) was of the opinion that the name should be read rather similarly as Yaho or Yeho (cf. his book *Die große Täuschung* [The Great Deception]) and was one of the first to suggest a Babylonian origin of the Old Testament, as argued in his book *Babel und Bibel,* published in English as *Babel and Bible* (Chicago: The Open Court Publishing Company, 1903). "I am that I am" might also imply, "It is none of your business who I am."

Other vowels have also been inserted into YHWH, which leads to other meanings (one such vocalization, *Yahaoah* (letter *vav* read as "o"), could even mean something like "bringing calamity").* So who is this god? Discoveries in the latter decades by research in the history of religion shed light on this. This is controversial, because this subject has very much to do with personal questions of faith and, therefore, requires a somewhat more extensive discussion.[17]

RESULTS FROM ARCHAEOLOGICAL FINDINGS

In recent decades, archaeological findings in the research into the history of religion have almost revolutionized our views about the origins of monotheism. It turns out that the Hebrew-Christian religion was originally polytheistic and even worshipped goddesses. In preexilic times (prior to the fifth century BCE), Asherah was primarily worshipped, but later, especially during the Babylonian exile (586–539 BCE), the religion of the Hebrews became a strictly dogmatic monotheism. Asherah, like other goddesses, was eliminated, and her symbols were destroyed in a drive toward patriarchy.

Unfortunately, these findings are still more or less unknown to the public. The church seems to ignore them, even though they are subjects of articles in scientific journals, theses, and symposia at university faculties for the history of religion. Here I will give a short overview of current findings, chiefly based on the extensive documentation of the symposium *Ein Gott allein?*

---

*If the letters are written in reversed order, HWHY, the Hebrew lexicon suggests that it could be composed of two words put together: HW = an outcry of sadness (like "Woe!") and HY = an outcry of lamentation (Gesenius's *Hebrew and Chaldee Lexikon*).

(Only one God?), with contributions in German and English.

These remarkable results do not indicate that there was no highest God, no primordial Creator, in the earliest monotheistic religions. But they do raise the question of whether our monotheistic religions actually relate to that primordial Creator, or whether they are pseudomonotheistic religions that relate to a kind of "intermediate god" that slipped into the original Creator's role (or was inserted into it for political reasons—by gods or by humans). As we have seen, Apsu, and not Anu or Marduk, is the original Creator in the Mesopotamian creation story—and in union with Tiamat! These two were devalued and in a way dethroned. Other gods pushed themselves in between them and us. The situation in India is a bit similar, although it is more open. There Parabrahman is held to be the one highest God, but no other deity tries to steal the show from him. If, for example, someone is devoted to Vishnu or Shiva, he knows that the deity is not the primordial Creator himself but, being itself created, in a way represents him.

The church and religious teachings have drummed into our heads the idea that there is only one God. Since ancient times, the god of the Old Testament is held to be the only one. In regard to this issue, Professor Walter Dietrich (Bern, Switzerland) writes in his introduction to *Ein Gott allein?:* "Is this image historically correct? . . . There are reasons that can be put forward for saying that the normative YHWH-religion at first was polytheistic. . . . In the town of Ugarit [today Ras Shamra] in northern Canaan, a manifold polytheism is discovered, with gods that are also mentioned in the Old Testament: 'El, Baal, Astarte, Anat and Asherah. While a peaceful coexistence and amalgamation of YHWH and 'El can be read into the biblical texts, Baal and the female deities are vehemently opposed." Dietrich mentions archeological findings in Kuntillet-'Ajrud (today Horvat Teman) and Khirbet-el-Qom (near Hebron), where inscriptions expressly mention YHWH and his divine spouse Asherah. "These extrabiblical textual testimonies have understandably engendered a great deal of turbulence among researchers," Dietrich explains.

This strict monotheism was formed during the exiles in Egypt and Babylon. And yet, he adds, "For a single god it is in a way more difficult to deal with all areas of the world and of human experience than it is for a pantheon. As a result . . . a multitude of semidivine entities became established. The figure Satan now comes forward . . . as well as an abundance of angels and demons. . . the semidivine figure of Lady Wisdom also belongs to this context." Her Hebrew name is Chokmah, in Greek Sophia.

Yahweh, a mountain god of the southern desert, became the personal and national god of the Israelites. That has left its traces in human history! Because strict monotheism can look like intolerance, fanaticism and fundamentalism followed as negative consequences. "It is not only in present-day times that Islam and, still more regrettably, Christianity are full of examples of how a 'belief in the god' can serve as an excuse for all hinds of evildoing, even genocide."[18] (This was written before today's misdeeds in the name of Islam, which are now overtaking those of Christianity.)

Both archaeological findings and the Bible attest that the original religion of Israel was characterized by worship of goddesses (e.g., Hosea 4:9–14, Jeremiah 44:15–19). Then this worship was defeated, and all was merged into Yahweh—male and female, good and evil, welfare and mischief.[19]

Some have wanted to see Yahweh as another name for the God 'El, "but this view is open for serious objections . . . whatever the exact origin of Yahweh may be, much indicates that he originally was the god of the mountain Sinai"[20] as well as a god of war.[21] 'El had seventy sons, the gods of the seventy nations of the Earth, and Yahweh was one of them—the god of one of these nations, namely Israel (Deuteronomy 32:8, Genesis 10).[22]

The assembly of god (or the gods) is mentioned in Psalm 82:1, 6: "God [*'Elohim*] standeth in the congregation of the mighty; he judgeth among the gods. . . . I have said, Ye are gods [*'elohim*]; and all of you are children of the most High [*'Elyon*]."

Of course, Yahweh is mentioned on almost every page of the Hebrew Bible; in all, 5658 times. *Yahweh 'Elohim* appears 40 times, *'Elohim Yahweh* appears 4 times, and *'Elohim* 680 times. Subtracting 44 from the last number, *'Elohim* alone is mentioned 636 times.

IS YAHWEH ENLIL?

In the Bible, Yahweh releases the Flood to wipe out a sinful humanity and to make a new start with Noah. (A kind of reset.) In the Mesopotamian texts, Enlil brings on the Flood in order to eliminate the whole of humanity, which has become annoying to him, while Enki transgresses a prohibition to speak, making a new development of humanity possible through Atra-Hasis (Utnapishtim, Ziusudra).

Yahweh is a god of war and storm.[23] The name *Enlil* means "lord of the storm," and he is also a god of war. His spouse is Ninlil (Sud). Enlil first rapes her and then seduces her twice, disguised as someone else, indicating a negative attitude toward femininity.[24]

Yahweh also first had a spouse, Asherah, who was apparently rejected and whose name was later not to be mentioned, so that it was covered up in the Bible. This too indicates a negative attitude to femininity. More is told about her below. Professor John Day (Oxford) alleges in his text "Yahweh and the Gods and Goddesses of Canaan" that Yahweh even may have had "affairs" with two other goddesses.[25]

Enlil is sometimes friendly to humanity but can also be severe, choleric, and even cruel. He punishes humans excessively and sends them calamities. Who does not recognize the biblical god in him? Some Mesopotamian images show him with a crown with horns.

THE "SONS OF GOD"

In Gen 6:2 and 6:4 we read "that the sons of God saw the daughters of men that they were fair; and they took them wives of all which they chose. . . . There were giants in the earth in those days; and also after that, when the sons of God came in unto the daughters of men, and they bare children to them, the same became mighty men which were of old, men of renown."

These "sons of god" are called "sons of the 'elohim" in the Hebrew text, that is, "sons of the *gods*" (*beney ha-'elohim*). From all that has been said here, it is highly probable that these 'elohim were actually the Anunnaki and were thus the aforementioned "watchers." The word that is here translated as "giants" is *nephilim,* and it actually means "those who fell down (or were thrown down)," from *naphal* = "fall" or "cast down." (The word *nephilim* is sometimes used as a misnomer for "the sons of the 'elohim," but in the biblical text it refers to their offspring with terrestrial women.)

Other translations refer to the "mighty men" as "heroes," "tyrants," and the like. They are *giborim,* also translated as "masterly men," humans with special capacities. "Men which were of old" (Hebrew 'olam) could indicate that they originated from beings that had been around for a very long time—again, probably Anunnaki.

After a long presence on the Earth, the Anunnaki left but retained control over us. For this purpose, they ordered some of their people (regarded as "angels" by the humans) to remain as "watchers" on our planet. Since (as mentioned previously) the Anunnaki are obviously multidimensional beings, they can hide in other dimensions, remaining invisible to us. Indeed, they probably engineered our DNA to limit our perception to three dimensions.

Although the Anunnaki apparently left us alone, the watchers became a link between them and us. But this was a one-sided communication and did not work the other way: we no longer received information about them, although they did about us. We did not know what was going on and did not have full control over ourselves. Instead they maintained a secret control over humans, subliminally and unconsciously. As is written in the books of Enoch:

And it came to pass, when the sons of men had increased, that in those days there were born to them fair and beautiful daughters. And the angels, the sons of heaven, saw them and desired them. And they said to one another: "Come, let us choose for ourselves wives from the children of men, and let us beget children for ourselves." And Semyaza, who was their leader, said to them: "I fear that you may not wish this deed to be done and that I alone will pay for this great sin." And they all answered him, and said: "Let us all swear an oath, and bind one another with curses, so not to alter this plan, but to carry out this plan effectively." Then they all swore together and all bound one another with curses to it. And they were, in all, two hundred, and they came down on Ardis, which is the summit of Mount Hermon. And they called the mountain Hermon ["fortress"], because on it they swore and bound one another with curses.[26]

So the watchers had children with the daughters of men that grew up to be giants. These allegedly took to devouring humans. They wanted to eat meat from them and from animals and drink blood. But these two hundred "fallen angels" also taught their children and the daughters of men many secrets about magic, astrology, geomancy, the use of metals, and other things. To god, this went too far, and he ordered Uriel to warn Noah that a deluge would come over the Earth. The fallen angels were then imprisoned in the abyss until the day of judgment.

In another text, the *Hebrew Book of Enoch* or *Enoch 3,* the watchers are also called *'irin* and *qadishin.*[27]

The *Book of Jubilees* tells us in chapter 5: "And against the angels whom He had sent upon the earth, He was exceedingly wroth, and He gave commandment to root them out of all their dominion, and He bade us to bind them in the depths of the earth, and behold they are bound in the midst of them, and are (kept) separate. And against their sons went forth a command from before His face that they should be smitten with the sword, and be removed from under heaven."[28] After that follows a description of a violent destruction, followed by the Flood.

The "sons of god" are mainly described in a negative way, but we may also have another impression of them. They had asked god not to "create" humans on the Earth, but since he had done so after all, they wanted to be close to them. The Anunnaki had "created" humans through genetic manipulation to make them work for them as slaves and wanted to keep them in a primitive state so that they would not understand too much and would remain compliant. It appears that the watchers had some compassion for these humans and wanted to raise their consciousness by giving them their own genes, and for that purpose they had children with terrestrial women (although their motives are described as pure lust). Thus the watchers violated a prohibition, which appears to be their real "sin." Humans were to be eradicated through a deluge because they were developing further than was intended (and they had eaten too much from the "tree of knowledge"). This actually means an *ethnic cleansing by god!*

Chapters 4 and 5 of the apocryphal text *The Book of Jubilees* even claims that the sons of the 'elohim had the *task* of educating humans and teaching them many things. They fulfilled this task (even if they might have gone a bit too far with it). Later they gave in to the temptation to become sexually involved with terrestrial women. What, then, was the real sin? Sexuality itself? Why, then, do both humans and, evidently, the watchers have sexual organs? Why should they have them but not be allowed to use them? After all, in Genesis 1:22 humans are told to reproduce. The logical answer is that this prohibition has to do with something else. The sons of the 'elohim were forbidden to have children with terrestrial women *because that way their genes would be given to humanity!* These genes led to a rapid but undesired development of humans on our planet. The Flood was intended to make them revert to an earlier state.

Could it be that the children of the watchers were "giants" in a different sense; that is, because they had a higher intelligence and a higher consciousness than humans were supposed to have (even if they may have also been bigger physically)? The accusation that these giants devoured humans (or perhaps made them captives) could be a defamation used as an excuse for their destruction.

The word *'Anaqim,* sons of Anak, is found in the Bible as a name for a population of tall humans in southern Palestine near Hebron and to the east of Jordan (the latter are also called Rephaim). The word *'anaq* means "necklace" or "long-neck." The Anakim allegedly wore neck chains and had long necks. It would not be far-fetched here to suspect an etymological connection with *Anunnaki!* The sons of Anak could also be connected with the Nephilim, even though the theologians do not like to see it that way. The name is found in nine passages in the Bible: Deuteronomy 1:28; 2:10–11; 2:21; 9:2; Joshua 11:21–22; 14:12; and 14:15.

BIBLICAL AND MESOPOTAMIAN GODDESSES

Now some may immediately object that there are no goddesses in the Bible. We will see. As mentioned on page 46, Yahweh originally had a spouse, Asherah. She is mentioned in various inscriptions from the earliest forms of Near Eastern religion. Some connect her with the Mesopotamian goddess Ishtar (Inanna), a daughter of Anu.

"In recent times a multitude of archeological data have been gathered together that indicate the existence of the Asherah cult of the old Canaanite mother goddess. . . . The efforts of some biblical scholars are revealing in the extent to which they try to circumvent such clear indications of Asherah being . . . his spouse."[29] Some strive to understand the word 'asherah as merely referring to some kind of a wooden figure connected with a cult, or even to a tree, without wanting to see a goddess who is symbolized by it. The word 'asherah occurs more than forty times in the Hebrew text of the Bible but is usually translated as "tree" or "grove." Archaeologist William G. Dever observes, "In at least half a dozen of these cases, the notion 'asherah' will refer to the goddess herself and not simply to a totem-like object. There is no way around it. These are Asherah figures."[30]

There is a certain grammatical problem here. In nineteen verses, the name appears with a male plural as 'asherim, in three verses with a female plural: 'asherot.[31] (The Hebrew masculine plural is -im; the feminine plural is -ot.) The male form will quite obviously refer to a wooden image or symbol of Asherah, while the female form refers to the goddess herself (together with her symbols, hence the plural). The name is derived from 'asher = "happy."[32]

There are verses in the Bible that appear to connect Asherah with Baal. That is an attempt to devalue her cult.[33] For some reason, those involved in the drive toward patriarchy did not want to have anything to do with her. It was forbidden to plant a "tree" at Yahweh's altar (Deuteronomy 16:21—the original text here has 'asherah). What sense could such a prohibition have unless the tree—or, perhaps better, a wooden figure—was a representation of Asherah? This wooden symbol is sometimes also described as a "pole," which could also involve a pun with the name Asherah. The root 'ashar, mentioned above, can indicate something that is "straight, upright" as well as "happiness, success."[34] Something that stands upright—a pole—could associatively serve as a symbol of Asherah. As a kind of defamation, some even suggest that such upright images would have been phallic symbols.

Regrettably, most modern versions of the Bible no longer contain a text entitled *The Wisdom of Solomon,* though this text can still be found in some specialized books of the Apochrypha. "In the wisdom books, the not easily interpreted figure Lady Wisdom appears; she may be understood as a goddess."[35]

The first Christians, the Gnostics, regarded the Holy Spirit as female. Many scholars want to connect this female Holy Spirit with Lady Wisdom—Sophia, Chokmah—who at some places in the Old Testament is even called "spirit of wisdom" (*ruach chokmah*: Exodus 28:3; Deuteronomy 34:9; Isaiah 11:2). According to an apocryphal text, Jesus talked about "my mother, the Holy Spirit."[36] Theologians want to explain the femininity of the Holy Spirit as a misunderstanding, on the grounds that the Hebrew word for "spirit," *ruach*, is grammatically female. That looks a bit like an evasion. In Judaism, the Holy Spirit corresponds to the Shekinah, the female presence of god, who has a special importance in the Kabbalah.

Another goddess is Anath, who is mentioned at two places in the Bible and in two more in the geographical name Beth-Anath (house of Anath), which probably indicates that Anath was once worshipped there. In Mesopotamia, she is Antu, one of the spouses of Anu. Ashtoreth, who is called Ishtar in Mesopotamia, is mentioned in three places as a false goddess (1 Kings 11:5, 33; 2 Kings 23:13). Athirat or Ashtoreth is, however, the Ugaritic name of Asherah (not to be confused with Ashtarte). The New Testament mentions Artemis (in some translations Diana) (Acts 19:27–37). Hence there is more divine femininity in the Bible than the advocates of patriarchy would like.

A special female entity mentioned in the Bible is Lilith.[37] She is seen as a female demon, and in Hebrew mythology, she was the first wife of Adam; she did not feel that he was treating her as equal and therefore left him. Then god (Yahweh) "created" Eve for him. Lilith is feared in Jewish folk belief because she steals children from their mothers after birth. She, however, also plays with children and makes them laugh. In the Bible, she is mentioned in Isaiah 34:14, where the Hebrew text calls her by her name, although translations usually render it as "screech owl," "night ghost," "female demon," "goblin," and the like. In Mesopotamia, she is a rather demonic but not entirely negative goddess, Lilitu.[38]

One may ask what the world would look like if the goddesses had not been banned from our principal religions. There is a soft, motherly femininity missing in our macho and patriarchal Old Testament Bible. The world might have been more peaceful and humane had this feminine element been preserved. Of course, the Virgin Mary has taken over some of this role, but she is not a goddess; besides, worshipping her seems to have contributed little to the salvation of the world. Even in politics, only "male women" seem to be tolerated. Maybe a return of the goddess is overdue.

3
GNOSTIC SPIRITUALITY AND THE ANUNNAKI

How False Gods Established Religion

A very short description of the creation as described by the Gnostic Christians is as follows (relying on the *Apocryphon of John*, also called *The Secret Book of John*).[1]

The First Being is invisible and unnamed and is described as an immeasurable light. He is eternal and indestructible. Through his will, a female companion, Barbelo (the etymology of her name is disputed; she is also called Pronoia or "providence"), emanated out of him, a light equal to him, the first thought, the primordial mother of the creation, the Holy Spirit. Through a spark from the First Being, the androgynous Autogenes ("self-begotten") appeared out of her, whom we call Christ.

Then out of the First Being and Christ the four aeons of light emerged to serve Christ. The last of them is Eleleth, to which, at the fringe of the divine perfection, belongs Sophia, Wisdom.

Sophia initiated her own creation, which in the end led to the material worlds. She tried to imitate the First Being and generated an entity out of herself, much as Barbelo had emanated Autogenes. Thus Sophia wanted to produce offspring, but without consulting with the First Being. Because a male element was missing, an entity came into being that, because of Sophia's imperfection, appeared like a dragon (or a serpent) with the face of a lion. She called it Yaldabaoth (probably from Aramaic *yalda bahut* or "son of chaos"). Shocked and shameful, she first hid it in a cloud and then threw it out of the Pleroma, the realm of divine perfection. It escaped to the lower regions. After that, Sophia, having lost the grace of the First Being, was called Norea. She later incarnated as a daughter of Adam and Eve. The sons Cain and Abel, however, were conceived because Yaldabaoth raped Eve. The first real child of Adam was Seth.

Here again, we have the issue of rape, which we have already seen in the preceding chapter: Enlil had raped his spouse, Ninlil. As we will see, Yaldabaoth is the Gnostic name for Yahweh. In Genesis 4:1 we read, "And Adam knew Eve his wife; and she conceived, and bare Cain, and said I have gotten a man from the LORD [Yahweh]." The Hebrew text could also, however, be understood as saying, "And Adam knew that she had become pregnant and bore Cain, and she said, 'I have acquired a man *with* Yahweh.'" A highly controversial interpretation, but it would fit the story.

Yaldabaoth stole power from his mother. Although he was still weak, he was ambitious and lusted for power. He emanated twelve entities, the archons, to rule in the nether regions that he had occupied for himself, and he also "created" 365 angels as assistants. In his arrogance, he boasted to the archons: "I am god and there is no other god besides me!" That is why he is also called Samael (the blind), because he did not want to see the truth. He is also called Saklas (the fool), a word that is sometimes connected with Satan. Gross matter manifested in his realm.

The world of Yaldabaoth is a world in the darker regions

where he let the stolen light of Sophia shine. For that reason, this world is neither bright nor dark, but dim. Those who live in it are used to the dim light and do not know that there is a brighter one.

Because of Sophia's regret, the First Being tried to save her distorted creation. The archons heard a voice and were frightened. They searched to find where the voice had come from, and Yaldabaoth saw a mirror image of the First Being in the "water" (an energy barrier between the divine world and Yaldabaoth's world) and tried without success to imitate it. Sophia's light became weaker, because Yaldabaoth had been able to take a part of it. Even so, she could make Yaldabaoth "create" Adam and infuse a part of his misappropriated spiritual essence into him.

When Yaldabaoth and the archons saw that Adam was essentially superior to them, they regretted having "created" him and wanted to get rid of him. But they could not, so they put him in the garden of Eden, an apparent paradise, where they allowed him to eat from the tree of life but not from the tree of knowledge, because it had to do with light forces from a higher world that Adam was not to know about.

Yaldabaoth then wanted to get hold of the light in Adam and take it out of him, but then Eve appeared, sent from higher regions. Adam saw a mirror image of himself in Eve and thus was freed from the ban of Yaldabaoth. It was Christ, who, through Eve's mediation, made Adam eat from the tree of knowledge.

Yaldabaoth then sought to regain control over the essence of the light. For that purpose, he launched the process of human reproduction, intending to generate new human bodies inhabited by fake spiritual forces. These fake forces were to seduce the human race and keep it in ignorance so that it would submit to him. This is the source of all evil and all confusion. It allows humans to die without having found the truth and without knowing the true God.

Some versions of the *Apocryphon of John* also mention the Flood. Yaldabaoth regretted having "created" humans, who in certain ways were superior to him, and for that reason wanted to let loose the Flood upon them.

So far we may establish the following hypothetical comparisons:

- The First Being and Barbelo—Apsu and Tiamat
- The fall of Yaldabaoth into dark regions—defection of the first Anunnaki
- Yaldabaoth turning away from the First Being and Barbelo to pose himself as "god"—the deicide of Apsu and Tiamat to make the Anunnaki turn away from them
- Apsu wanting to reverse the "creation" of humans—Enlil's disdain for the humans, wanting to reverse their "creation"

Kishar, the third goddess (after Tiamat and Lahamu) in the *Enuma Elish*, is also regarded as "Mother Earth." Could she be compared to Sophia? Again, there is very little information about her in the Mesopotamian texts, so this will be rather speculative. In any case, she was there before the Anunnaki, and she was the mother of Anu. Hence she was the grandmother of Enlil, whose mother, Ki, was one of the spouses of Anu. Alternatively, she may be connected with Norea, Sophia after she had fallen from grace.

A comparison of the Gnostic texts with Genesis 2 makes it obvious that Yaldabaoth is identical to Yahweh (and hence Enlil). He and his archons are the Anunnaki. This explains the monstrous cruelties carried out in the name of god in the Old Testament.

When comparing the Old Testament with Mesopotamian

texts, one should keep in mind that the Bible is pro-Yahwistic and paints a positive picture of everything having to do with Enlil/Yahweh, while the Gnostic texts are critical of Yahweh and thus paint him in different colors. Therefore the latter texts will, using their own terminology, describe creation processes before the emergence of Yaldabaoth/Yahweh that other texts leave out or that were withheld from the scribes.

A HYPOTHESIS ABOUT YALDABAOTH

Origen, a church father of the second and third centuries, was not a Gnostic but stood close to them. His worldview compares well with those of the Gnostic Christians and may be seen as complementary to them.[2] According to Origen, there are twelve levels in the universe. The highest level is the divine light of the primordial Creator. Below that are nine angelic hierarchies.[3] The eleventh level is that of the humans, and the twelfth is the level of demons and adversaries.

According to Origen, we in the beginning were all on the first and topmost level as children of light, who then developed and grew up. After time, many of these children became weary of existence in the light, which had become monotonous for them (only light and love and nothing else . . .). Therefore they wanted to go out of the light to have experiences that they could not otherwise have.[4] They especially wanted to fully live out their free will, which had been given to them by God, and the possibilities for doing so in the light were limited. The light beings were so closely connected—and yet individual—that they partook directly of the others' feelings. If a child of the light did something that hurt another, it would immediately feel the pain of the other being (a kind of instant karma). For that reason, they did not do all that they could have done, but some wanted to try out other possibilities. This was another reason for them to want to go out of the light. The Creator God said something like, "This is not a good idea, but because you do have free will, I will let you have it." Then he contracted himself, generating a region outside of the light. This region grew increasingly dark the further it proceeded from the light. (Compare the Kabbalistic idea of *tzimtzum,* "contraction" or "constriction.")[5] In that region, new worlds formed, especially the eleventh and twelfth levels mentioned above (that is, those of the humans and the demons). A large number of those who wanted to go out from the light became souls and were put into bodies like prisons.[6] After this, through reincarnation they went from one embodiment to another until they became mature enough to return to the light world and stay there without having to incarnate again.

One may then ask if the emergence of Yaldabaoth really was an accident in the creation, because the Creator God could hardly let a mistake occur. As an answer to this question, I had the following intuitive inspiration, which I want to describe here as a hypothesis. In the beginning, the darker regions were empty, and some kind of organization or structure was needed before the light children could go there. For that purpose, a suitable administrator needed to come into existence, but it could not be a light being from a higher level, because then the outer region would no longer be truly dark. To serve as a first barrier between light and dark, an entity was needed in whom the light was concealed and who was unconscious of it (just as it is for all of us in this dark region we live in, but we do not know it: when we are used to the dimness and know nothing else, it seems to be light to us). This entity was Yaldabaoth, who first went out in the darkness and made worlds there where light children could dwell. Since light is life, we all have the light inside, or we would not live, but most of us do not know it.

YALDABAOTH
AND JESUS

As stated on page 59, Yaldabaoth is seen as an "accident" in the creation, an *error*. He is literally called this in the Gnostic text *The Gospel of Truth*: "Through this, the gospel of the one who is searched for, which [was] revealed to those who are perfect through the mercies of the Father, the hidden mystery, Jesus, the Christ, enlightened those who were in darkness through oblivion. He enlightened them; he showed (them) a way; and the way is the truth which he taught them. For this reason, *error grew angry with him, persecuted him, was distressed at him, (and) was brought to naught.* He was nailed to a tree "[7] (emphasis added). Jesus knew and told too much about truths that Yaldabaoth wanted to conceal from us. For that reason, Gnostic Christianity, which had arisen out of the inner circle around Jesus, was later combated as well, and its texts were concealed until a large number of them were found again in Nag Hammadi, Egypt, in 1945. When Jesus talked about the Father, he doubtless did *not* mean Yahweh, but the highest Creator.

CAN CHRIST BE FOUND IN THE
MESOPOTAMIAN TEXTS?

Here is a problem. In the Mesopotamian texts, the prehistory before the creation of the Anunnaki (missing from the Bible) is discussed very briefly, and Christ would obviously have existed before them. The only entity in that story that might be compared to Christ would be Mummu, who appeared directly out of the primordial Creator pair, Apsu-Tiamat. The Mesopotamian texts say almost nothing else about him, however, so a comparison is not possible. Since the *Enuma Elish* and other texts only tell the story about the Anunnaki, and Christ (Autogenes) in a way that is outside of the story, it could well be that he is never mentioned in these texts, just as parallel lines of development that led to other civilizations are not mentioned either. The tree of creation has a number of branches that are unknown to us.

Even though the *Enuma Elish* initially describes Mummu as a rascal, we need to see this in the light of the above-mentioned reversal of good and bad that appears to be a tactic of the Anunnaki. Tablet 7 describes Mummu as the creator of heaven and Earth (rather than as a collaborator with Apsu and Tiamat) and as a helper and protector of humans, who sanctifies and maintains heaven and the underworld. In any case, there is a trinity in each instance: Apsu–Tiamat–Mummu; First Being–Barbelo–Autogenes; and God–Holy Spirit–Christ.

WERE THE GNOSTICS REAL CHRISTIANS?

As for Gnostic Christianity, there are two schools of thought in today's theology (according to the renowned German reference work *Theologische Realenzyklopädie*):

■ The conventional German school assumes that the Gnostic Christianity arose out of a pre-Christian gnosis and therefore is not truly Christian.

■ The Anglo-Saxon and French schools, however, regard the idea of an origin in a pre-Christian gnosis as speculative. Their position is *that none of the texts allows for the assumption of a pre-Christian gnosis, nor of any preceding stages.*[8]

Today the German view has come closer to the latter as a result of epoch-making works by Carsten Colpe. It is possible even to speak of a certain sympathy (although a limited and furtive one) for Gnostic Christianity among modern theologians.⁹ Therefore it can no longer be said that the Gnostic Christians were not real Christians.

Characteristics of Gnostic Christianity:

- A radical dualism that regards this world as evil and under the rule of hostile powers.
- A differentiation between the unknown, transcendental, and true God and the demiurge or "creator" of this world (Yahweh).
- A view that humans are, in their true nature, essentially equal to the divine.
- A myth of an antediluvian fall that explains the current condition of humanity.
- A belief that humans achieve liberation by means of insight into their own true nature and its heavenly origin through gnosis.¹⁰

The last feature, by the way, has nothing to do with the "self-liberation" that is despised by ecclesiastical theology—a belief that certain movements, especially of an esoteric nature, have been accused of. Such self-liberation cannot exist, because true liberation can only be achieved by means that are established by the highest God. How else could it be liberation?

The word *gnostic* comes from the Greek word *gnorizo,* which means *to make known.* Hence it literally means *knowing Christians.* In contrast, one is tempted to call the others *ignorant Christians* (or, using a modern expression, to talk about a "Christianity lite").

The Pauline doctrine, then, is not only a deviation from what Jesus taught, but also relates to the *outer* circle around him, in which certain important things were not said: "I have yet many things to say unto you, but ye cannot bear them now" (John 16:12).

Before Paul began his preaching, another Christian movement was growing vigorously—Gnostic Christianity. This *original Christianity* related to the *inner* circle around Jesus, as the Gnostic texts that were rediscovered in the twentieth century attest. Hence the Gnostic Christians knew many things that Jesus did not mention when he spoke in public, but said only to his disciples. The Gnostic Christians were the ones Paul fought against when he still called himself Saul.

WHO IS THE DEVIL?

The word comes from the Greek *diábolos* = slanderer, accuser, but also "divider" and "one who throws through." He is often called Satan, from the Hebrew *satan* = opponent, adversary, accuser. Who is he?

In Job 1:6 he is mentioned as one of the "sons of the 'elohim" In *The Book of the Secrets of Enoch* (also called *The Second Book of Enoch*),[11] he is called Satanael (Satanail) and is said to be one of the "watchers"[12] (Nephilim)[13] that were thrown down from heaven.

Three quotes to ponder:

God's terrible concealment, experienced as unclearness and uncertainty, is due to his being the source of evil *and* good (Lamentations 3:38), life *and* death, light *and* darkness (Isaiah 45:7), happiness *and* unhappiness (Amos 3:6). Beauty and cruelty are to us inextricably tangled in nature and history.[14]

According to their critics, these heretics referred to the Abrahamic God variously as "a demiurgus," "an evil angel," "the devil god," "the Prince of Darkness," "the source of all evil," "the Devil," "a demon," "a cruel, wrathful, warlike tyrant," "Satan" and "the first beast of the book of Revelation."[15]

As for the paradoxical statement that both come from YHWH: light and darkness, salvation and calamity (Isaiah 45:7)—does it solve the problem, or does it give up in front of it?[16]

What is the problem that is mentioned here? The problem of good and evil, especially of evil. How can Yahweh be *both*? Is he his own adversary? Since he already poses as the "creator," he could also hijack the role of the opponent. As if "you need neither a god nor a devil, only me, because I am both." A clever move!

The Bible and other texts say that Satan was a vain and arrogant angel who thought of himself as being greater than God and for that reason was thrown out of the divine world of light into darkness. This has parallels to claims in various texts that Yahweh and Satan are actually one and the same, so that one could understand Satan as a concealed face of Yahweh. The arrogant angel could well be the Yaldabaoth of the Gnostic Christians.

The devil, be he called Satanael or Satan, was thrown down because of his arrogance: "For thou hast said in thine heart, I will ascend into heaven, I will exalt my throne above the stars of God: I will sit also upon the mount of the congregation, in the sides of the north: I will ascend above the heights of the clouds; I will be like the Most High" (Isaiah 14:13–14).

Here a question intrudes: are Satan and Yahweh identical—as some Gnostic texts may suggest—or is he one of the archons? After the fall, he could have become an archon that is closely tied to Yahweh. The following intuition comes to my mind: together they play an intriguing game. Satan appears as an opponent to Yahweh for the Machiavellian purpose of *divide et impera*—divide and conquer. There could be two ways: the way of Yahweh and the way of Satan, which lead to the same end, and many are going there by one route or the other. In that case, it would be a clever tactic, invoking a freedom of will that in the end is nonexistent. Could that be the answer? In that case, none of the ways is the true one; the true one is rather, in a manner of speaking, the way that takes off over their heads.

WHO IS LUCIFER?

The King James Bible reads in Isaiah 14:12: "How art thou fallen from heaven, O *Lucifer*, son of the morning! How art thou cut down to the ground, which didst weaken the nations!" (emphasis added). Luther's version says (translated from the German): "How art thou fallen from heaven, you beautiful *morning star*! How art thou felled down, you that weaken the heathens!" Other translations have *shining star*, *day star*, and *shining one*; most have *morning star* and the like. Only few translations have *Lucifer* here.

The Hebrew word that is here translated as *Lucifer* or *a star* is *heylel*, "the shining one," derived from *helal* = shine (but also "boast" and "be foolish"). Isaiah 14:12 more accurately has "[you] shining one, son of the dawn (or morning)." The association with the morning star is an interpretation; so is the translation "Lucifer." What is meant by the "shining one" is not clear. Lucifer is nowhere found as a name in the Bible. Indeed *Lucifer* (carrier or bringer of light) is merely the Latin translation of *heylel* and not even a name. In the Greek New Testament, the translation is *phosphóros* (bringer of light) or *heosphóros* (bringer of dawn). Certain ancient texts have "son of Shahar." In the pantheon of Ugarit, Shahar is the god of dawn, and his brother, Shalim, is the god of dusk. They are sons of El and are regarded as gods of Venus.[17]

And one from out of the order of angels, having turned away with the order that was under him, conceived an impossible thought, to place his throne higher than the clouds above the earth, that he might become equal in rank to my power. And I threw him out from the height with his angels, and he was flying in the air continuously above the bottomless. *The Book of Secrets of Enoch* (also called *The Second Book of Enoch*) 29:3–4.[18]

Compare Luke 10:18: "And he [Jesus] said unto them, I beheld Satan as lightning [*astrapé* = bright light, flash] fall from heaven." Here the Greek text has *Satanas,* but it remains a question which word Jesus actually used in his language. The Greek word is a translation from an Aramaic text that we do not have.

Is there, then, a difference between Satanael, Satan, and the one who is called Lucifer? I found a possible hint here: "Satanel (The unfallen Lucifer) had the Secret Wisdom, Satan corrupted it."[19] Could Satan then be the fallen Lucifer?

In Bogomilism, a Gnostic movement of the late first millennium CE, Satanael was held to be the "creator" of the physical world, with all its misery and suffering. He "created" Adam and Eve. He then "assumed the form of a serpent and had sexual intercourse with Eve with his tail, begetting the twins Cain and his sister Calomena."[20] He oppressed humanity and told them that they should worship him instead of the true God—very much reminiscent of Yaldabaoth.

Here Satan and Lucifer become mixed up. It is a confusing game that should obviously not be easy to understand.

WHAT ABOUT ANGELS?

The word "angel" comes from the Greek word *ángelos* = "messenger, envoy," in Hebrew *mal'ach*. Angels are usually considered to be either male or sexless, the latter mainly because of what Jesus said in Mark 12:25: "For when they shall rise from the dead, they neither marry, nor are given in marriage; but are as the angels which are in heaven." Being unmarried, however, need not mean sexlessness. Female angels are mentioned in Zechariah 5:9: "Then I lifted up mine eyes, and looked, and, behold, there came out two women, and the wind was in their wings; for they had wings like the wings of a stork: and they lifted up the ephah between the earth and the heaven." (An ephah is a measure of volume as well as the vessel used for measuring, but in Hebrew, it could also be the feminine form of a word for "darkness.")

The angel Gabriel is occasionally held to be feminine (Gabriele, Gabrielle) even though this idea is taboo in patriarchal theology. Some regard this angel in a not very positive light because he (or she), according to the Islamic tradition, forced Muhammad (then still an illiterate) with physical violence to read and write the Qur'an. On the other hand, it was Gabriel who in Luke 1:26–38 appeared to Mary to inform her about the coming birth of Jesus. For that reason, some hold that there are two different entities, and that in the story about Muhammad a demon posed in the shape of Gabriel (Jibra'il). The Gnostic text *Pistis Sophia*[21] mentions that Christ (Autogenes) took on the appearance of Gabriel in order to keep from being recognized by the archons of Yaldabaoth, thinking he was Gabriel, and that he then "found Mary, who is called 'my mother,' after the material body; I spake with her in the type of Gabriel."

Some authors seemingly assimilate the concept of angels with that of extraterrestrials in general, especially to the Anunnaki. This may apply to the watchers, or to the archons of Yaldabaoth, and the "angels" that were "created" by him. These may be regarded as fallen angels, but no doubt there are also a large number of light beings in higher regions as well as benevolent multidimensional extraterrestrials.

WHO ARE ENKI AND ENLIL?

So who are the gods Enki and Enlil? As Parks[22] and others show, it can hardly be doubted that Enlil is the one who is called Yahweh in the Bible. Who, then, is the more benevolent Enki? It has been suggested that he could be Lucifer; in that case he is obviously to be distinguished from Satan.

According to Parks, *shatam* in Sumerian means a major administrator for the region of the gods; in that case it would apply to Enlil. Now it becomes a bit confusing.

Slave Species of the Gods by Michael Tellinger[23] is an interesting book, although in writing about Enki, he refers to Sitchin's *The Lost Book of Enki,*[24] which Parks[25] and others correctly regard as an invention.

Tellinger writes that Enlil opposed "creating" humans on the Earth and wanted to eradicate them with a deluge.[26] But since many survived—through intervention by Enki, as the clay tablets relate—Enlil wanted to keep humans undeveloped, ignorant, and stupid so that they would obey without asking too many questions.[27] Wanting to be their god, he attempted to control them by means of fear, intimidation, and bloodthirsty power. Since he put himself higher in rank than Enki, he felt free to do what he wanted with the humans, who had been "created" by the latter. Because of this conflict, he defamed Enki, portraying him as a snake and a devil, and forbade humans to have anything to do with him. Yet Enki, eluding the prohibition, has taught humanity to raise its consciousness in various ways.

It seems that things have been deliberately tangled in order to make it difficult to see through them.

As far as Lucifer and Satan are concerned, I believe that they are *not* one and the same, but that Yahwistic interests want us to believe that this is the case, because Lucifer is in reality an opponent to Yahweh. Satan would then be a hidden face of Yahweh himself. It has been claimed that Lucifer is not really evil but has been portrayed as such for political reasons: because he brought knowledge and illumination (hence "light-bringer") that humans were not supposed to have. Thus he thwarted Yahweh's plans.

What is alarming in this context is that there are various human orders that call themselves Luciferian, but who in their rituals, magic, and even sacrifices appear outright Satanic. (Some information about this can be found on the internet.) Some such orders scandalously designate themselves as "Luciferian Gnostics" (who are in no way to be confused with Christian Gnostics!). Again, the impression is that the two names *Lucifer* and *Satan* have been jumbled for tactical reasons. Nevertheless, a few of these orders, at least at first glance, give the impression of being honest and morally decent. Such obscurity and disorientation are no doubt in the interest of Yahweh and a pseudo-Christian church in order to make people believe that Lucifer and Satan are one. Is this a game of Yahweh meant to cause uncertainty and confusion? Such games may even have led to two concepts of Lucifer: one that is autonomous, and one that is identical with Satan.

It is disquieting that there are increasing rumors of Satanism in the Vatican. An Italian book *Via col vento in Vaticano* ("Gone with the wind in the Vatican") was published in 1999 under the pseudonym "I Millenari" and caused much agitation. A whole group of people who belong to the church are said to hide behind this pseudonym for protection. There was a court action against them, but only one could be identified. In 2001, another book by the group was published as *Fumo di Satana in Vaticano* ("Smoke of Satan in the Vatican"). These books allege that secret satanic rituals and worship are performed in the Vatican.[28] It is said that nuns stole the book from Italian bookshops, because they did not dare to buy it openly.

The Exultet prayer in the Vatican at Easter is disquieting: "Flammas eius lucifer matutinus inveniat ille, inquam, lucifer, qui nescit occasum, Christus Filius tuus, qui regressus ab inferis, humano generi serenus illuxit, et tecum vivit et regnat in saecula saeculorum."[29] Translated: "May these flames be found by Lucifer, I say, by Lucifer of the morning, who never sets, Christ your Son, who has returned from the depths, has shed his peaceful light on humanity, and lives and reigns with you in ages and ages." Is Satan actually meant here, meaning that the two are one and the same? Or is this related to the intentional name confusion mentioned above?

It has been objected that *Lucifer* here refers to the "morning star" (or "day star") and as such refers to Christ. Therefore, we actually have two meanings of "morning star": Lucifer and Christ. (For the latter, see 2 Peter 1:16; Revelation 2:22, 28; and 22:16.) For the faithful, it could only mean the latter, but in view of the discussion above there is room for doubt, especially since there are not a few Satanic symbols in the Vatican, including even a cross in the pope's chair that is *upside down*![30]

Satan fell out of the divine world, and so did Yaldabaoth = Yahweh. Sophia fell from the grace of the First Being and brought light in the darker regions; she was then called Norea. Is Yaldabaoth the same as Satan, and does Norea have to do with the real Lucifer? Since Lucifer is also called Venus (the morning star), that may fit.

Therefore we may assume as a hypothesis that Enki, who thwarted certain plans of Enlil/Yahweh, could be a benevolent bringer of light. It has been suggested that Enki and Satan could be one and the same, but this does not fit well with Enki's character. It seems more fitting to see Enki as someone who brings light and to assume rather that Enlil and Satan are one and the same. To bring light into darkness should actually be good. If someone had been sent here with such a task, Enlil/Yahweh might be expected to defame him as a devil. Even though Enki appears more benevolent, this does not, however, mean that he would not play his part of the game in his own interest. This could be another trap on the path.

Although we have some food for thought here, we cannot get much further than to leave the connections and relations among these figures as an open question, but we should consider these things: *every devil wants to pose as a god, and every god calls his opponent a devil.* It is the same game on both sides. The image of an enemy is politically useful because fear is such an effective tool for manipulation. When humans are afraid, they will allow anything to be done to them.

WHO ARE THE ARCHONS?

Much has been written and said about the archons in Gnostic Christianity. Who are they? Yaldabaoth is called the chief archon, and he "created" seven archons to serve him. They are also called the Hebdomad, "the seven." The word *árchon* is Greek and means "high officer" (although, in another context, it also means "origin" or "principle"). These archons are agents of Yaldabaoth, working with him in his "creations." The archons "created" seven powers and 365 angels. (In that case, the latter do not really belong to the angels of light.) They are spiritually primitive and envy humans for our souls, abilities, and talents (even though we use these only to a limited extent). They want to restrict our abilities, obstruct our activities, and manipulate us so that we will not eat from the tree of knowledge (see pages 26 and 56). They maintain a false world in which they want to shield us from the true reality. An important aim in Gnostic Christianity is to bypass the archons after death and go beyond and above them, since they want to keep us in this world to incarnate here again. They also feed on our life energies and emotional energies.

This description makes it clear that the archons are Anunnaki.

THE SYMBOLISM OF THE SNAKE

The snake or serpent is usually seen as a symbol of evil, but it is also a symbol of wisdom, life, and medicine, and of fertility and protection of holy places. Enki's symbol is two snakes intertwined with each other in a spiral fashion. In the Bible, the snake urged Eve to eat from the tree of knowledge, after which she and Adam opened up spiritually. In the *Apocryphon of John* it is written:

But what they call the tree of knowledge of good and evil, which is the Epinoia of the light. . . . it was I [Christ] who brought about that they ate.

And I [John] said to the Savior, "Lord, was it not the serpent that taught Adam to eat?" The savior smiled and replied, "The serpent caused them to eat from wickedness of begetting, lust, (and) destruction, that he (Adam) might be useful to him. And he (Adam) knew that he was disobedient to him (the chief archon) due to light of the Epinoia which is in him, which made him more correct in his thinking than the chief archon. And (the latter) wanted to bring about the power which he himself had given him. And he brought a forgetfulness over Adam."

And I said to the savior, "What is the forgetfulness" And he said, "It is not the way Moses wrote (and) you heard. For he said in his first book, 'He put him to sleep' (Gn 2:21), but (it was) in his perception. For also he said through the prophet, 'I will make their hearts heavy that they may not pay attention and may not see'" (Is 6:10).[31]

This could also involve limiting their perception to three dimensions.

Some want to connect the snake in the Garden of Eden with Enki.[32] Be that as it may, the quotation from the *Apocryphon of John* indicates that the snake does not necessarily symbolize evil but has a double sense, because the snake acted according to the will of Christ.

The quotation is reminiscent of another pseudepigraphal Old Testament text, *The Life of Adam and Eve*,[33] here shortened: The devil told the snake that he had heard that it would be cleverer than other animals. He had a plan to have Adam and Eve be driven out of the paradise. The snake replied that it feared the wrath of god. The devil reassured it by saying he would speak through its mouth. Eve then saw the snake hanging on the wall around paradise. It asked Eve what she ate. She replied that she ate everything except from the tree in the middle of the paradise. The snake lamented her foolishness and said that if humans would eat from it, they would become like gods; god had forbidden them to eat from it because he was jealous. Then Eve let the snake come into paradise. It did not want to let her eat from the fruit before she swore that she would also give it to Adam to eat. The snake poisoned the fruit with greed and wickedness and gave it to her. When Eve had eaten it, she discovered that she was stripped of the righteousness that had before surrounded her like glory. All the leaves of the trees had fallen down, and only the fig tree (the tree from which she had eaten) had kept its leaves, from which Eve made an apron. She called Adam and persuaded him that he would be like god and realize good and evil, and he ate. Adam now understood what had happened and reproached Eve for it.[34]

It is impossible to say which word in the no longer extant original Aramaic text has here been translated as *devil*. In comparison with the Gnostic text the *Apocryphon of John,* one may assume that there is the tactical reversal of good and evil here, since the author of this text obviously was convinced that the true god was Yahweh/Enlil. Whoever is against him and wants to liberate Adam from being lulled into a sheeplike drudgery will therefore be a devil from his point of view. (The devil is always the one on the other side.)

As Tellinger writes: "After having a run-in with his brother Enlil about the upliftment of Adam and Eve, the creator of humanity, Enki, realized that the slanderous campaign against him as a serpent, and the evil snake, would be fiercely enforced by Enlil."[35]

That the message mediated by the snake turned out to be true is confirmed in the Bible itself: "And the LORD God said, Behold, the man is become *as one of us,* to know good and evil" (Genesis 3:22; emphasis added).

In Hebrew, *nachash* is a word for "snake," but it also means "interpret," "find out," "decipher." *Saraph* denotes a poisonous snake. From this word is derived *seraphim,* signifying a class of shining angels, actually "winged snakes" (an etymology that is disputed, maybe because some do not like it); *nachesh* (differently vocalized) also means "shining." (Cf. *heylel* and *helal* above. Here one may again speculate.)

A fringe movement in Gnosticism, the Ophites or Naassenes (cf. *nachash*),[36] held the snake in high esteem because it had outsmarted Yahweh in Eden and led Eve and Adam to wisdom. And the so-called "tree of knowledge," when correctly translated from Hebrew, actually means "tree of wisdom"!

Jesus said "Behold, I send you forth as sheep in the midst of wolves: be ye therefore wise as serpents, and harmless [simpleminded, Greek: *akeraios*] as doves" (Matthew 10:16). Who wants to defame the Gnostics only because of the snake rather acts like simpleminded doves.

DISTORTIONS
OF GNOSTICISM

As mentioned on page 69, today one can find distorted forms of Gnosticism that designate themselves as Luciferian Gnosticism. They have nothing to do with the original, true Gnostic *Christianity*. There is a great deal of disinformation around about Christian Gnosticism, obviously in an attempt to defend established power systems and deflect threatening truths. Only the old Gnostic texts from the first centuries can be taken seriously. Even in the early centuries, somewhat different versions of Gnostic Christianity developed. One is the Sethian Gnosticism, which relates to Seth, the third son of Adam and Eve (see remarks on page 55 about Cain, Abel, and Seth). Some slanderers want us to believe that he would be the ancient Egyptian god Seth, widely regarded as a figure of evil.

4

JESUS'S MISSION

The Christ and the Antichrist

There were *two* circles around Jesus: (1) the *outer* circle of people who heard him speak, and (2) the *inner* circle of his disciples and others who were close to him. John 16:12 shows that there was much that he did not say in the *outer* circle but doubtless said in the *inner* circle: "I have yet many things to say unto you, but ye cannot bear them now."

Out of the inner circle arose Gnostic Christianity (which preceded Paulinian Christianity), because the very first Christians in that circle must have included at least a few of the earliest Gnostics. As is written in the *Gospel of Truth,* Yahweh was enraged because of what Jesus taught and had him nailed to a cross. This has already been discussed on page 60. Why was Yahweh enraged? Because Jesus said that Yahweh is not the true God; according to the Gnostic text *Pistis Sophia,* he even told how we can become free from Yahweh's influence.[1]

Yahweh expected that Jesus's teachings would gradually be forgotten, but the opposite happened. Jesus's sacrifice gave his teachings more power, and they were carried on by the Gnostic Christians. For that reason, Yahweh wanted to replace the original Christianity with a new one that would serve his purposes. He brought Paul to establish a "Christianity lite" that no longer had the deep truths of the Gnostic Christianity or Jesus's teachings in the inner circle, but merely told us what Yahweh wants us to believe.

In this manner, the original Christianity was gradually replaced by Paulinian Christianity. Yahweh manipulated the Roman emperor Constantine to reject Gnostic Christianity at the council of Nicaea in 325 (the theme of the council was another, but some Gnostics were present and were not allowed to speak). At this point Paulinian Christianity became the basis for the church that developed afterward.

Acts 9:4–6 reports about the conversion of Paul: "And he fell to the earth, and heard a voice saying unto him, Saul, Saul, why persecutest thou me? And he said, Who art thou, Lord? And the Lord said, I am Jesus whom thou persecutest: it is hard for thee to kick against the pricks. And he trembling and astonished said, Lord, what wilt thou have me to do? And the Lord said unto him, Arise, and go into the city, and it shall be told thee what thou must do." (Paul probably fell to the ground because he had epilepsy. In folk belief, this was considered to be a sign of demonic possession.)

Did this really come from Jesus, or from Yahweh posing as Jesus? Let us compare this with another vision. It is said that Constantine had a vision (some sources say a dream) in which he saw a cross and heard a voice saying, "By this sign you will conquer." He then had the cross (a tool for torture and execution!) painted on his soldier's shields and won the war he was fighting. Did that really come from Jesus? Jesus taught us, "Thou shalt not kill," "Love your enemies," and "All they that take to the sword shall perish by the sword," flagrantly contradicting the vision of Constantine. Jesus would have told him to make peace and reconcile with his enemies! Hence that vision cannot have come from him. Did it come from Yahweh, who wanted to have an *apparently* Christian Church as a tool for manipulation and control of the people? If so, it also raises doubts about the vision of Paul.

We may then in the same sense ask who it really was who tempted Jesus in Luke 4:1–13. Could it have been Yahweh, trying to divert him from his mission?

Yet the Gnostic Christians did not completely disappear. Some Gnostics remained in the Balkans, in present-day Bulgaria, and they later spread to southern France, where the community of the Cathars was formed. The Cathars ("the pure ones") followed Jesus' teachings to such an extent that they were vegetarians and did not even kill animals ("Thou shalt not kill"!). In my opinion, they were the most Christian people since Jesus's disciples. In the thirteenth century, this community was completely eradicated in a holocaust by the men of the church. An *extremely unchristian action*! It was one of the greatest sins of the church, along with the Inquisition, which in its cruelty worked as Yahweh would have liked, as well as the Crusades, not to mention the many wars it stirred up.

The Cathars also knew about, and taught, the doctrine of reincarnation. As concerns reincarnation, we could imagine that it is hinted at in John 16:12.

The Gnostic texts were destroyed in an attempt to annihilate this movement. Luckily, many of them were found in Nag Hammadi in Egypt in 1945 so that we again have access to a major part of this treasure of very important information. Did that happen according to the will of the original Creator to save the truth for our time?

A RESPONSE TO
MICHAEL TELLINGER

Michael Tellinger has written a valuable book, *Slave Species of the Gods,* about the origin of humanity. But in chapter 5 he writes that "Jesus became an unwitting mouthpiece for his bloodthirsty Nefilim god, preparing the ground for the continued enslavement of humanity . . . unconsciously weaving the propaganda of a power-hungry Anunnaki god. . . . The uncanny parallels between the murky origins of humanity, compared to the origins of Christ, point to the real possibility that whoever crafted humanity followed it up with a second wave of premeditated, calculated propaganda and ultimate control."[2] He could not have written this if he had known about the Gnostic Christians and their texts.

His subsequent remark is also untrue: "The one truly puzzling feature is the lack of reference to the messiah in the Old Testament. The word *messiah* first appears in John 1:41." Since the Hebrew word for "messiah," *mashiach,* is usually translated as "the anointed one," used for someone who is chosen by God for a specific task, we have to search for the latter in the Bible. This expression is found in eighty-four passages in the Old Testament. and in some of them it may be understood as it is in Christianity. What is most remarkable, however, is that Tellinger writes about "origins of Christ" (see above), even though in his opinion no such origin can be found in the Bible.

The Bible and ecclesiastical Christianity have hypnotized us to identify Jesus with Christ, which has led to many misunderstandings. The Jesus of Christianity, for obvious reasons, was unknown before his birth in Bethlehem. The name *Yeshua* was given to him, just as any name is given to a newborn child. But who was he before he took incarnation? That we do not know. Therefore it is logical to expect that no Yeshua can be found in the Old Testament who could be the one of Christianity. (At least two persons named Yeshua are mentioned in Old Testament apocrypha: Yeshua ben Sirah and one in "The Book Yoshua," but only the names are the same.)

But Christ is not a *name*! It is the Greek translation (*christós*) of the word *mashiach*, "the anointed one," that has been adopted in almost all modern languages. Here there is much confusion. As mentioned, *mashiach* is in most cases not used in the Old Testament in the "Christian" sense. That sense was unknown to those who wrote those texts. It mainly became known to us through his message, brought to us through Jesus.

What, then, was the explosive part of Jesus's message? As mentioned above, it was that Yahweh is not the true God! There is one high above him, whom Jesus called "Father." Yahweh is an Anunnaku, but the Father is above all Anunnaki. Of course, delivering such a message in those days put one in mortal danger, and it is obviously the reason that Yahweh wanted Jesus to die.

This means that we effectively have two Jesuses: the real one and a pseudo-Jesus of the church. Since Yahweh could not completely eradicate his message, he twisted it to serve his interests. The first step was to put Paul on stage to teach a modified Christianity. Out of that, a church evolved as an institution to manipulate the people with another "Christianity" and make them believe that Jesus's father was Yahweh. John 8:31–47 quotes Jesus as speaking in front of the people (see below) in a way that contradicts this, but as can be expected, it is interpreted in another way by the church.

There are, therefore, also *two Christs*: the real one, who sent us Jesus as his messenger, and a fake Christ established by the dogma to serve the politics of a church that effectively has become secular.

In a way, what Tellinger writes is actually true—but of the fake Jesus of the church and not of the real Jesus.

Tellinger repeatedly refers to Sitchin's books. Sitchin has obscured important passages in the *Enuma Elish* and played them down. Sitchin seems to revere the Anunnaki as true creators—did Sitchin, then, have an unconscious contact with the Anunnaki? In his interpretation, Apsu would be the Sun and Tiamat a planet that broke to pieces a very long time ago. But these figures can also be understood literally: Apsu can be seen as the primordial Creator and Tiamat as his female partner (who gave "birth" to the creation). These two are, then, the very first beings, by whom and out of whom the universe was created. Apsu may be mythologically *associated* with the Sun, but to *identify* him with it is another thing. Tiamat may be mythologically *associated* with a no longer existing planet, but *identifying* the two is, again, another thing. One reason to emphasize this becomes clearer when we compare it with the creation story in the *Apocryphon of John*[3] (as was done on page 54).

In my understanding, the Father that Jesus spoke about is the unnamed Creator of the Gnostics and Apsu of the Mesopotamians, who is above all the Anunnaki—and not Yahweh!

JESUS'S MAIN MISSION

The first mission of Jesus that comes to mind is *love*. He taught us that love is more important than anything else and that we are all brothers and sisters in this world, irrespective of origin, race, gender, culture, or social status. This is the most important touchstone for those who call themselves Christians. If they are able to live this love, seek no revenge, cannot hate, are never violent, and even love those who regard themselves as their enemies, then they can truly call themselves Christians. How many pass this test? Probably only a handful of all those who claim this name.

What is love? It is to want the best for all involved, not only for oneself. It is a fundamentally positive and helpful attitude to our fellow brothers and sisters, while not allowing others to abuse us. It excludes violence, but in case of an attack allows for defense—whether of someone else or of oneself—by means that are as peaceful as possible. Love also includes honesty, justice, and mutual respect. Much more can be said, but this brief definition will be sufficient here.

There is, however, another and still more important mission for which Jesus came into this world: as a messenger of Christ. For many even today, this mission may appear controversial, and yet it was for this reason that he was killed. No one can imagine that he was killed because he taught love. It would have had to be something else for which the powers of this world wanted him dead.

We can learn about this in the Bible, if we have eyes to see and ears to hear and are prepared to accept his mission. We learn about it from the first major Christian movement in this world, the Gnostics.

We have testimony in John 8:31–47 in the Bible:

Then said Jesus to those Jews which believed on him, If ye continue in my word, then are ye my disciples indeed; and ye shall know the truth, and the truth shall make you free.

They answered him, We be Abraham's seed, and were never in bondage to any man: how sayest thou, Ye shall be made free?

Jesus answered them, Verily, verily, I say unto you, Whosoever committeth sin is the servant of sin. And the servant abideth not in the house for ever: but the Son abideth ever. If the Son therefore shall make you free, ye shall be free indeed.

I know that ye are Abraham's seed; but ye seek to kill me,

because my word hath no place in you. I speak that which I have seen with my Father: and ye do that which ye have seen with your father.

They answered and said unto him, Abraham is our father.

Jesus saith unto them, If ye were Abraham's children, ye would do the works of Abraham. But now ye seek to kill me, a man that hath told you the truth, which I have heard of God: this did not Abraham. Ye do the deeds of your father.

Then said they to him, We be not born of fornication; we have one Father, even God.

Jesus said unto them, If God were your Father, ye would love me: for I proceeded forth and came from God; neither came I of myself, but he sent me. Why do ye not understand my speech? even because ye cannot hear my word.

Ye are of your father the devil, and the lusts of your father ye will do. He was a murderer from the beginning, and abode not in the truth, because there is no truth in him. When he speaketh a lie, he speaketh of his own: for he is a liar, and the father of it.

And because I tell you the truth, ye believe me not. Which of you convinceth me of sin? And if I say the truth, why do ye not believe me?

He that is of God heareth God's words: ye therefore hear them not, because ye are not of God. (Emphasis added)

About whom did Jesus speak the words that are italicized above? And who is it that he calls his "Father"? There is only one meaningful way to understand this. The "father the devil" is Yahweh! Jesus's Father is a God *higher* than Yahweh, the true origin, the original first Creator, in whose creation Yahweh is a lower-level entity who pretends to be the only god.

These words about Yahweh are based on facts in the Old Testament. Jesus himself said, "I will open my mouth in parables;

I will utter things which have been kept secret from the founda-
tion of the world" (Matthew 13:35). That is what Yahweh did
not like: Jesus came to tell us things that Yahweh wanted to keep
secret, especially the truth about Yahweh himself.

Jesus was born to a people that Yahweh, through Moses, had
led to the promised land. After a long wandering through the
desert of Sinai, they finally reached that land, only to find, to
their disappointment, that it was not empty. People lived there
in towns. Therefore Yahweh ordered them to kill everyone without exception, not sparing a child, a woman, or an old man, so
that they could live in "houses full of all good things, which
thou filledst not, and wells digged, which thou diggedst not,
vineyards and olive trees, which thou plantedst not; when thou
shalt have eaten and be full" (Deuteronomy 6:10–11). They con-
ducted a holocaust in which they attacked one town after the
other and let none remain, as is vividly described on the bloody
pages of Deuteronomy, Joshua, Judges, and other books of the
Bible. By means of this genocide, they stole the land from its
original inhabitants in order to have it for themselves. Is that the
work of a loving and peaceful God, like the one Jesus called his
Father? This bloodthirsty, revenging, hating, murdering, punish-
ing, lying, and threatening god? Of course not!

Yahweh had already shown his cruelty as they wandered
through Sinai. One example is reported in Numbers 16:35–49.
Yahweh killed 250 men for offering incense. The people pro-
tested, and as a punishment for doing so, he let 14,700 persons
die from a plague.

In Numbers 31:14–18 we read: "And Moses was wroth with
the officers of the host, . . . which came from the battle. And
Moses said unto them, Have ye saved all the women alive? . . .
Now therefore kill every male among the little ones, and kill
every woman that hath known man by lying with him. But all

the women children, that have not known a man by lying with him, *keep alive for yourselves*" (emphasis added). Numbers 31:35 says that they came from a raid and brought 32,000 virgins as booty, but all the others were killed. Why should all these girls be left alive? Doubtless for sexual services.

A few more examples. Numbers 2:34–5: "And we took all his cities at that time, and utterly destroyed the men, and the women, and the little ones, of every city, we left none to remain [survive]. Only the cattle we took for a prey unto ourselves, and the spoil of the cities which we took." Hosea 13:16: "Samaria shall become desolate; for she hath rebelled against her God: they shall fall by the sword: their infants shall be dashed in pieces, and their women with child shall be ripped up."

In the Psalms we read:

18:38: I have wounded them that they were not able to rise: they are fallen under my feet.

21:9–12: Thou shalt make them as a fiery oven in the time of thine anger: the LORD shall swallow them up in his wrath, and the fire shall devour them. Their fruit [children] shalt thou destroy from the earth, and their seed from among the children of men. For they intended evil against thee: they imagined a mischievous device, which they are not able to perform. Therefore shalt thou make them turn their back, when thou shalt make ready thine arrows upon thy strings against the face of them.

137:9: Happy shall he be, that taketh and dasheth thy little ones against the stones.

There are so many examples of this kind that they could fill a book of its own. An extensive account of Yahweh's cruelties can be found on the Skeptic's Annotated Bible website.[4] An interesting text is, "Who Is the Real God of the Bible?"[5] Two books about this issue are *Jehovah Unmasked!* by Nathaniel Merritt,[6] and (in Spanish) *Desenmascarando a Yahweh* (now also in English as *Yahweh Unmasked*) by David Cangá Corozo.[7] Merritt writes:

> Human beings are victims of a race of elohim/archons, or "gods" that fashioned this material universe, and humankind, out of dead defiled pre-existent matter. "In the beginning the gods created the heavens and the earth" *(Genesis 1:1),* and humans remain their possession to this day. To maintain control over humans, and to make sure Earth continues as our dungeon, the elohim/Archons have made this Earth a continual source of endless squabbles amongst humankind. They have created and fostered religious and spiritual delusions to keep us blinded to reality and fighting and warring with each other, and they have made Earth into a place of relentless pointless physical and mental suffering and struggle. This sorry state of affairs has existed from the beginning, lost in the mists of prehistory.[8]

Is it not obvious that all this disqualifies Yahweh—who ruled over the land of Canaan and today rules over the whole world through churches that have accepted him as their "god"—from being the true God? When he says, "Thou shalt have no other gods before me" (Exodus 20:3), does that mean that there are no other gods, or is it a restraint of trade, forbidding competition? Is it meant in the sense, "There are other gods, but I shall be your only god and you shall have nothing to do with them"?

About the logic of this statement: If Yahweh had been the original Creator, he would have created the other gods, and he would probably have nothing against humans' worshipping them. If he does, they are not his creations. In that case, they would have been created by another Creator, who, then, is obviously higher than Yahweh. Hence, Yahweh too was created by that higher Creator.

A SUMMARY HYPOTHESIS

- Jesus is not Christ, but a messenger sent by Christ.
- There are effectively *two Jesuses* and *two Christs*: the true ones and the fake ones established by the church through manipulation by Yahweh.
- Jesus passed his mission on to his disciples so that they would spread it in the world. Thus Gnostic Christianity came to be—the first and original Christianity. Part of its teaching is that Yahweh is a fake god.
- This aroused wrath and hatred in Yahweh, who had Jesus murdered, hoping that his teachings would be forgotten. That did not happen. They were carried on by the Gnostic Christians. To counteract this, he used Paul to establish a modified Christianity to serve his interests.
- Then Yahweh also wanted to get rid of the Gnostics. For that purpose, he used Constantine to erect a church based on Paulinian pseudo-Christianity and declare Gnosticism a heresy.
- The Gnostic texts were destroyed, but an important collection of them was hidden and discovered in Nag Hammadi in Egypt in 1945. This is unlikely to be a coincidence, but rather part of a plan by the primordial Creator to restore the original teachings.

Nonetheless, it appears that Jesus did not break the power of Yahweh or liberate humanity from his rule, because the situation became worse afterward. Yahweh's power and influence became stronger. In this respect, the same questions may arise concerning both Jesus and Christ. Did he actually serve Yahweh (as Tellinger claims) and not the Father about whom Jesus spoke? Or did they fail? Or is this a process that takes a very long time by human measure, but is still in action and is now coming into its last phase?

The first question is in any case valid for the *fake* versions of Christ and Jesus; that is, they were both used to serve the interests of Yahweh. This would not be the case for the true Christ and the true Jesus if the process is still going on, but in that case, it is a matter of a human misunderstanding that is intentional.

If the latter is true, Yahweh will know that his days are counted and will want to tighten his power over the humans more than ever before he has to give up. As his last action, he may want to destroy as much as possible of this planet and its population—scorched-earth tactics.

Yahweh is an extraterrestrial: he and his associates do not belong to the humanity of Earth, but to other dimensions in another world, with another civilization. For millennia, that civilization has established an invisible control over us. They claim to have "created" us, but that is not true. They have only modified existing life-forms and have implanted a few chosen genes of their own in us. In no way are they our creators. The only thing that they could do is to manufacture a small group of the ancestors of present-day humanity on the Earth by genetic means. After that, no further humans were manufactured but were procreated by us. These extraterrestrials therefore have no right to control or make use of us. Yet they do it in order to feed on our life energies (invisibly to us and out of our scope of consciousness), as if we were energetic "cattle" for them.

Over the course of many millennia, humanity has been manipulated by extraterrestrials who established different religions as tools for control. Some were benevolent. The manipulative ones, especially those begun by Yahweh, wanted to destroy their competitors and created a fake Christianity to do so. An invisible war is on, but in the future there will arise a new humanity, supported by beneficent extraterrestrials (and not by the New World Order, which wants to prevent that). Humans will have to die by huge numbers in this process—but *there is no death*. Only the body dies. The immortal soul leaves and comes back at a later time—into a new humanity.

WHO IS THE
TRUE ORIGINAL CREATOR?

There can be only one true Creator, the one who was called 'El 'Elyon (the highest God) by the Canaanites. Canaan, an essential part of the promised land, was inhabited by people who knew the truth, mainly from Mesopotamian sources, as has been confirmed by findings in excavations. Enlil = Yahweh, mentioned by these sources, wanted to keep this truth hidden from humanity so that he could pose as the only god. That seems to be why Yahweh led the Hebrews back to Canaan and ordered them to eradicate its population. Why did this happen, and how had they come to Canaan in the first place?

The Origin of Judaism was the covenant between Abraham and Yahweh (Genesis 15). Abraham and his family lived in Ur in Sumer. The Bible tells in ancient versions that their ancestors had generations earlier come to Sumer from the East (Genesis 11:2). After the covenant, Yahweh led them, the original Hebrews, from the city of Ur in Chaldea to the region of the land of Canaan (Genesis 11:28–31), where they obviously preserved Mesopotamian knowledge. Much later, many of them were led to Egypt because of a famine (Genesis 12:10). There they were treated as a secondary class, and Yahweh used their misery to lead them back to Canaan, ostensibly for their salvation. Did he do all this to eradicate the ancient knowledge through a mass brainwashing or an ethnic cleansing? He actually had the Hebrews kill their relatives, descended from the same ancestors.

Many later versions of the Bible state that the ancestors of Abraham would have come from the West, indicating that they originally may have come from Canaan and then returned there. An interesting book supports the hypothesis that the origin of the Hebrews was Sumerian and questions from where they had originally come: *From Sumer to Jerusalem: The Forbidden Hypothesis* by John Sassoon.[9] (I vainly searched for this book in several European university libraries and had to buy it. The hypothesis is apparently forbidden in the academic world.) It shows that the Hebrews in Ur probably did not come there "from the west," as most of today's Bible translations allege, but moved westward to come to Ur, that is, from the East. From Persia?

However that may be, they brought culture and knowledge to Canaan that had originated in Sumer, or even earlier, still further East. Their culture contained a religion with knowledge about Yahweh and his own origin that was problematic for his ambitions to usurp the role of being the one and only god. Therefore it was in his interest to eradicate this culture and replace the population with those who had lost this knowledge during their generations in Egypt.

WHO IS ANTICHRIST?

Antichrist somewhat generically means someone who is against Christ and his messenger, Jesus. (One could also say *Antijesus*.) According to all that we have seen above, the main candidate would be Yahweh.

YAHWEH AND REINCARNATION

Antonio Orbe (1917–2003) was a major authority about Gnosticism. He wrote as follows:

> Christ did not take seat to the right of Yahweh only to be revered by the heavens. As appreciation for his services (and for the death on the cross), a new order was established—throughout the whole New Testament—that was contrary to the previous rule. It was not a matter of preaching the Gospel to the angels and archons. The revelation of the Father is connected with the Son, the savior. Nor was it a matter of replacing Yahweh in his function of demiurge. Strictly speaking, this function continued under a new aspect. The "creator" did not manufacture new worlds, and he did not shape new humans.
>
> What was the task of Christ in establishing this new order? Not all Gnostics reply in the same way, but most of them agree about one essential thing: Christ took reincarnation to an end. He weakened Yahweh and revoked his rule over all who believed in the Gospel of Jesus and liberated them from the cycle of rebirth.
>
> During the Old Testament, Yahweh came and, at the root of death, took power over all humans, pagans and Israelites, good and evil, and obliged them to take on new bodies on the Earth as humans. In such a way, they go from one generation to another without hope of breaking the chain of births. A subterranean hell was superfluous. It was useless to gather the dead in one place. It was sufficient to oblige them to live again in new bodies and under other circumstances (of family and region) without leaving the Earth. Even the good ones had to pay their duties to the demiurge and to the cycle of birth into which he placed them. Thus the soul of

Phinehas [cf. Numbers 25:11] came back in the body of Elijah and later in the one of John the Baptist. There were even Gnostics who were tempted to seek the history of the fate of Adam's soul (or inner man) in his reapparitions and reincarnations. . . .

The destruction of such a rule was declared with the arrival of Jesus in the world and with his triumph over fate. . . . But it was completed after the return, when Messiah took seat on the right side. Sitting to the right of Yahweh, with power over him, Christ (as an entity) liberated all who were devoted to the gospel of truth. No one of those who confessed to God the Father and the Savior as the only-begotten Son would fall into the fatal circle of rebirths. In their postmortem journey, all of them would be liberated from the hands of Yahweh and go into the hands of Christ.

The disbelievers, who, insisting on the ancient beliefs, continued to worship Yahweh as the only true god, would remain under the rule of the Old Testament. They would continue to reincarnate, going from one body to another through death. Whoever refuses the advantage of salvation (and submission) that Jesus brought to the world is punished by continuing to be a slave of Yahweh and his arbitrariness, and thus in this world feeds the mass of his worshippers through *metensomatosis* [reincarnation]. They would never experience Christ sitting at the right hand as a means for salvation for the good of humanity.[10]

This does not mean that Yahweh introduced reincarnation into his realm. It was always there. The belief in it (or rather the knowledge about it) is as old as humanity and belongs to almost all cultures and religions, including the original Gnostic Christianity and essentially to the Hebrew religion as well. Even Islam had and has groups believing in reincarnation. Instead Yahweh hijacked it for his purposes. He wanted to keep the souls in his domain, and for that to happen, they had to reincarnate in it. For that purpose, he wanted humans to be violent and wicked in order to create bad karma for themselves and so ensure their return to his domain. This works better if people do not believe in reincarnation. Thus Yahweh strove to eliminate the knowledge about it in his religions. That is why this belief has been lost in the churches and in Islam, as it has been in the Hebrew religion (even though knowledge about it remains in the Kabbalah). This does not mean that Christ immediately liberates those who believe in him from reincarnation, but that he, through his messenger Jesus, showed us *the way out of it,* by which we can greatly shorten the circle of rebirth and escape it sooner. (Most of us will have some residual karma to work out.) Obviously Yahweh did not like that.

5

EATING FROM THE TREE OF KNOWLEDGE

Sexuality and Other Extraterrestrial Influences on Human Culture

The Gnostic Christians, as well as Origen and others, taught that our true origin is in the light body of the original Creator. We all come from there, and we were all there before we were embodied for the first time. We go back to this light after death, but at first only to a fringe region, because we have to come back here for new incarnations until we really understand love. After a final incarnation, we can go back into this light fully and stay there.

In embodiment, we are separated from one another by the physical shells that surround our consciousness. There is no such separation in the light world. There we are directly connected to one another, while remaining individuals. When we have come so far that after a final incarnation we no longer need to go out from the light (cf. Revelation 3:12: "He shall go no more out"), there can obviously no longer be such separation. That means that we must overcome the separation *before that*. The way to do this is through love, because it bridges what separates. Benevolence and positive feelings for one another eliminate separation; hatred and negative feelings reinforce it. Violent actions, deception, and dishonesty reinforce separation even more. Someone who is still living in the separation is not yet mature and cannot go completely into the light.

KNOWLEDGE AND SEXUALITY

We discussed the tree of knowledge a few times above. The conventional dogmatic understanding is that "eating" from it is sexuality. This myth requires a closer analysis. Here are some reasons for believing that the Bible does not refer to sex as the original sin:

- Adam was forbidden to eat from the tree *before* Eve was created, when sexuality was not yet an issue.
- They ate from the tree *separately,* Adam after Eve. Sex is done together, not by one after the other.
- Eve did not become pregnant then, but later (Genesis 4:1, see page 27).

It seems that the apparent connection with sexuality is supposed to distract us from the fact that this is in reality a matter of forbidden *knowledge.* As mentioned above, the Hebrew term is more correctly translated as "tree of wisdom." In Genesis 1:28, we are told to reproduce diligently; besides, we were given sexual organs, so it really cannot be forbidden to use them. The only question is how. Sexuality in true love is different from simply manifesting lust (certainly so if without conscious and full consent from the persons involved), especially when it happens in a kind of intoxication of the senses. In that case it is quite easy for invisible entities to join in, manipulate us, and nibble at our sexual energies. This is the only real problem with sexuality.

The Cathars did not regard sexuality as sinful in itself. They disapproved of it because it leads to the birth of children, so that souls have to incarnate in this evil world. (There was little or no contraception at that time.)

Today's media connect sex with materialism and even violence and make it look as if it has nothing to do with love, or they even identify sexuality itself with love. The woman is pictured as a sex object and the man as a macho stud bull. There seems to be a desire to devalue or cover up the true meaning of sexuality. This meaning does include reproduction, but it is not limited to that. True sexuality has to do with love. It is a union of the souls of two human beings, even when reproduction is not intended. Love that is sexually expressed also helps to bridge separation. In today's overpopulated and materialistic world, the latter sense is becoming increasingly important.

OTHER EXTRATERRESTRIAL INFLUENCES ON HUMANITY

As has been mentioned, the *Enuma Elish* and other creation stories leave open the possibility that there are other gods and other worlds, populated with humans and civilizations, in the universe. These regions are outside of the Anunnakian domain in which we live. Have any of these others visited the Earth and left traces behind? The sudden appearance of high cultures that later disappeared again could easily lead us to speculate about "development aid" from beyond this Earth, even though this help is unlikely to have been given without self-interest.

Scientists, with their limited worldview, deny the existence of Atlantis and Lemuria but cannot present real evidence against it: it cannot be true because it is not *allowed* to be true, because it does not fit the consensus worldview. And yet there is evidence that these cultures really existed and may even have experienced extraterrestrial influences.[1]

There is a large number of publications and internet sites about this subject. Here I will only briefly mention a few examples and give a brief overview.

HINDUISM

There are reports in age-old Indian texts about flying vehicles (*vimanas*, "celestial wagons")[2] and many other strange things. Sanskrit texts describe how various machines, even flying machines, are built.[3] The *Mahabharata* and other ancient writings describe terrible wars that mainly take place between vimanas in the sky with weapons that are in many cases reminiscent of modern nuclear weapons.[4]

The caste system in India still exists today. Could this have an origin in humans who were tailor-made for special functions—as the Anunnaki did in Mesopotamia and the Near East? And over the course of millennia, did these castes intermix with one another so that there is no real difference among them anymore, except what is maintained by tradition and imposed social codes?

These and many other reports suggest, in my view, that the Indian gods could have come from space. Hinduism is in a way henotheistic but ultimately monotheistic, because it refers to one highest God, Brahman (neuter) and Brahma (male). Brahman is the unmanifest form of the original Creator, and Brahma his manifest appearance. He first created two gods, Vishnu and Shiva, who then themselves created further gods (divinities, *devas*) or manifested in other shapes with other names (usually called incarnations of higher gods). Most of these gods also have spouses at their side—goddesses. Thus, for example, Krishna is an incarnation of Vishnu, and his spouse is Radha.

One may get the impression here that these are other extraterrestrials than the Anunnaki, and that the ones they were combating could well have been Anunnaki. Indian theology also speaks of demons, called *asuras*. Even an extensive Sanskrit dictionary gives no etymological explanation for the word.[5] Could it have something to do with Assyria? The Assyrian name for *Assyria* is *ashshur*. Could the asuras actually have been Anunnaki in Assyria?

Some may object that this hypothesis (which is admittedly speculative) is nonsense on the grounds that *a-sura* is the negation of *sura* = *god*. But this is incorrect. A Sanskrit dictionary explains: "by false etymology fr. *as-ura, understood as a negative:* a-sura."[6] The word *sura* (supposedly meaning "god") is a folkloristic construction out of an erroneous etymology, and thus *asura* is not a negation.

A video on the internet reports about recently discovered underwater ruins, adding to the mystery.[7] These ruins are from the town of Dvaraka, which until now was held to be a myth.

EXTRATERRESTRIALS IN MESOAMERICA

Many other cultures and religions also indicate the possibility of extraterrestrial origins. The Incas tell about Viracocha, who came from the Milky Way and later went back there. He is supposed to return to the Earth in the future. The feathered serpent of the Aztecs, Quetzalcoatl, reminds one of the Anunnaki in his thirst for blood and his demand for human sacrifices. The Norse god Thor (Þórr) traveled in a vehicle over the sky, described in a way that could make us think of an extraterrestrial sighting. These are just a few examples.

The Mayan name for Quetzalcoatl was Kukulkan, and the Maya too sacrificed humans to him (see the discussion starting on page 31 about how the Anunnaki feed). But in this case, we may be dealing with the Maya as seen through an Aztec lens. According to regression experiences of people who had past lives in these times, the history of the Maya looks quite a bit different from what official historiography tells us. They were a peaceful, vegetarian people who traded with the Aztecs and other tribes. They referred to the Aztecs as "blood-drinkers" and did not like them but had to barter with them for goods they needed. Some 2,100 years ago, Aztecs invaded the Maya country and forced their religion upon them. A small group of Mayans escaped to the sea on rafts. Many drowned, because the rafts were too quickly tied together and the cords were loosened by the seawater. The rest reached Florida, where they lived for some time and then died out.

THE EGYPTIAN CULTURE

The double star Sirius[8] and the constellation Orion[9] play important roles in Egyptian religion and mythology in relation to the gods. Some representations show the pharaoh Akhenaton[10] and others in ways that do not resemble terrestrial humans very much. Hypotheses about extraterrestrial relations with ancient Egypt have been built on these issues.

Enigmatic elongated skulls have been found in Egypt and other parts of the world.[11] What do they mean? Some of these skulls are not only very long but are also bigger than is normal today. Other long skulls appear to be a bit smaller. That leads me to the following thought: could it be that the watchers (see page 47) were the real giants, but their offspring with terrestrial women were not so big? Another fact to consider is that in some cultures parents tied the skulls of children to compress and lengthen them. Why would they do that? To make them look like extraterrestrials whom they knew and regarded as gods?

The downfall of the Egyptian culture is mysterious. Could it have to do with extraterrestrials leaving them on their own so that humans could no longer sustain the culture?

TIBETAN BUDDHISM

Tibetan Buddhism is very different from the original doctrine of Siddhartha Gautama—also called Shakyamuni or the Buddha ("the illumined one" or "the awakened one")—which in many ways is a philosophy rather than a religion. In Tibet, unlike in the original Buddhism, a number of divinities are known. Could they possibly have to do with extraterrestrial influences? Theodore Illion (1898–1984) was, by his own account, in Tibet in the 1930s and wrote two books about his experiences there.[12] In his book *In Secret Tibet,* he writes about large subterranean regions under a part of the country where humans are supposed to live who could possibly be of extraterrestrial origin. Similar stories are told in a text called *The Disks of Baian-Kara-Ula*[13] in relation to peculiar archaeological findings that are called the Dropa stones.[14] Be that as it may, these are speculations, and the possibility of extraterrestrial influence remains open.

The Russian explorer Nicholas Roerich[15] also wrote about a subterranean world in Tibet.[16] So did Lobsang Rampa,[17] although he is not regarded as an authority on Tibet, because the name is merely a pseudonym for the English-born Canadian Cyril Henry Hoskin (1910–81), who claimed to be the walk-in of a Tibetan monk.

WERE THE WORKERS BRED BY THE ANUNNAKI THE FIRST HUMANS ON THE EARTH?

Official science estimates that there have been humans on the Earth for some 1 to 2 million years. In his book *The Cosmic Code,* Sitchin claims that the Anunnaki came here 450,000 years ago.[18] In that case, there would have been humans on Earth at least 500,000 years before that, maybe much longer. The Anunnaki, then, would have been confronted with already existing peoples when they bred their humans. This may have been like extraterrestrial encounters with populations in later times, although there are no accessible historical accounts about this. It is only in relatively "modern" times that the Anunnaki have successfully globalized their secret subliminal influence.

6

ARE THE ANUNNAKI STILL HERE?

Secret Societies and Artificial Intelligence

Those who are spiritually more open, who occupy themselves with these questions, and who can think beyond the rim of the dish on which the conventional worldview is served usually assume that the Anunnaki never really left the Earth. Even if most of them withdrew several millennia ago, some remained here for surveillance and in order to influence us in their interests. Enlil and Enki obviously belong to these. They want to expand their influence as far as possible over all of humanity. First Enlil used the opportunity to gain the attention of a people that were treated as a secondary class in Egypt and made use of them for his interests. As has already been mentioned, he used them to eradicate the Canaanites in order to suppress their knowledge about the highest God. Later, he strove to widen his influence over the world by means of a modified Paulinian Christianity and the church that arose out of it. This was quite successful, but, in the long run, not to the extent that he wanted. Therefore he later established a parallel religion, called Islam. It is true that in both religions "god" is one and the same, but not fully, because neither of them worships the *highest* God. It was in Enlil's interest to see which of the two ways he could use to better control humanity. Also it is occasionally useful for him to play the two against each other in a Machiavellian way.

Enlil also wanted to eradicate other religions that had partial origins in other, competing extraterrestrial civilizations. For that purpose, he made use of Christian offensives through colonization and missionary activities among various populations, as well as religious wars. The great indigenous American cultures were conquered and destroyed, as were the Celts, the ancient Nordic culture, African populations, and others. In India and East Asia, Enlil had less success with the church, but more with Islam. He even used the latter to displace the influence of the church, which served him less well than it had—not least because ancient Christian truths had gradually surfaced that he wanted to keep suppressed.

And if Enlil and other Anunnaki, who were operating at the time, are no longer in their multidimensional bodies, they could still do mischief as discarnate entities; for example, by influencing others who continue to play these games in their interests.

However hard such allegations are to digest (and this has to do with instilled emotional resistance rather than with real facts), it seems that a cosmic war between the Anunnaki and more benevolent extraterrestrial cultures is still going on. This is a conflict over a subliminal, but increasingly obvious, manipulation of humanity that appears to have two aims: to establish complete surveillance over us and to drastically reduce the Earth's population to a size that is easier to control. For the latter, various measures are used: increased mortality by means of diseases and intentional environmental pollution with manipulated food and chemtrails as well as through pharmacology, but also reduction of population growth through decreased fertility (through pharmaceutical manipulation; for example, with adjuvants in vaccinations). For these purposes, in most countries governmental power has been handed over to an "elite" who are members of essentially secret organizations such as the Illuminati, Zionists, Bilderbergers, and Masonic lodges like Skull & Bones that have been established for this purpose. This elite probably only partially consists of conscious quislings.

Another present phenomenon is refashioning sexuality so that it no longer serves the purpose of reproduction. Alternative forms of sexuality are popularized in present-day gender ideology, which promotes sexual activities that cannot lead to pregnancy. I do consider homosexuality an accepted lifestyle in our society. Male and female homosexuals are just as much our brothers and sisters as anyone else, particularly in a Christian sense. But if such a lifestyle is (at least indirectly) *promoted* through the media, there is no doubt a hidden agenda of sex without children behind it. This is still more the case with the establishment of a large number of "genders," like transsexuals in various roles (who, nonetheless, are still our brothers and sisters). The common core education that is now spreading in the Western world includes a sexual education that is obviously intended to confuse the future sexual orientation of our children through exposing them, almost from infancy, to things they cannot possibly understand yet.

For decades, there have been reports about a highly secret cooperation between the extraterrestrials and the U.S. military to develop new and more powerful weapons and to manipulate humanity biologically and psychologically. Among the better-known whistleblowers are Phil Schneider and Milton William Cooper, author of the book *Behold a Pale Horse*, who were both murdered for their disclosures, and the still-living Fritz Artz Springmeier (alias Earl Schoff).[1] A special book in this context is *UFO Highway* by Anthony F. Sanchez.[2] It could well be an invention, but so far it has impressed me as reasonably plausible. If most of these statements are essentially true, by 1940 the U.S. military had already discovered the presence of a subterranean population of an extraterrestrial origin and later began to cooperate with them. This has to do with the "grays," extraterrestrials who, like present-day Earth humans, are allegedly another "creation" of the Anunnaki, used to serve them in various tasks, such as surveillance of Earth humans. They would have a technology that is developed far beyond ours. It is said that one could access historical records of these grays and discover that there is another "race," the *tall whites*, descendants of the Anunnaki who once were on the Earth. These Anunnaki would have had problems with the living conditions on our planet—for example, our atmosphere would not be well suited to their biology, and they would not have been fully resistant to human diseases. Therefore they had genetically adapted their own people (the ones who remained here), resulting in a kind of Anunnaki mutation— the tall whites. The original Anunnaki on the Earth are said to have died out as time went on; these whites would then have taken over. They have supposedly been here for millennia and are almost indistinguishable from Earth humans externally, but they are supposed to have the real power in the world, and function as a shadow government that rules over world governments behind the scenes. Nevertheless, because they are not perfectly adapted to living conditions here, they want to reshape the Earth to make it fit them better so that they will not die out as well. Do they need genetically modified food and chemtrails in the air? Are nuclear catastrophes in some way suitable for them? There is a suspicion that they tolerate radiation well and even may be able to feed on it energetically. Edward Snowden, who became famous for his revelations of the American surveillance state, has also given information about these tall whites.[3] It is in no way astonishing that the media reacted to these statements with ridicule. Another person who has given information about such things is the former Canadian minister of defense Paul Hellyer, whom it is a bit more difficult to ridicule.[4] Some readers may dismiss such information immediately, but a more sensible attitude is to at least hear it and think about it. Only then can we come closer to an objective judgment. After all, ridicule is an age-old method of cover-up.

Hellyer has said something that other sources have also claimed: positive extraterrestrials do not intervene in the mess on our Earth, because they respect our freedom of will. That is strange, because in that case they would be respecting *the freedom of will of the evildoers and not of the victims*. To put it in an exaggerated way: "I will not save your life, because I respect the free will of your murderer." That is unacceptable, and it simply cannot be that way. The only possibility is that so far the negative extraterrestrials are still stronger. But karma may also be playing a certain role in the victims' fates.

The book *UFO Highway* claims that the origin of the Anunnaki (or their ancestors) would be a planet near the double star Sirius. If that is true, there would have lived a people of "gods" on that planet, who later "created" the Anunnaki. These "gods" would have discovered our solar system and come here millions of years ago. It is not known why they left Sirius. They first settled on Mars, where most of their colony was destroyed by the impact of an asteroid (maybe a chunk of the broken planet Mallona or Phaeton; see page 18), and then continued on to the Earth 350,000 years ago. Here the Anunnaki emerged out of them 250,000 years ago. This description differs from that in the *Enuma Elish* and does not mention an original creator God. Apparently no planet is mentioned in the history of the grays that could be identified with Nibiru or Planet X, and the author of *UFO Highway* merely refers to what Sitchin has written about it. But it may be possible to link the two stories to each other somehow.

The hypothesis that Nibiru could be our Moon and could actually be a kind of spaceship could explain how the "gods" came here from Sirius and then from Mars to the Earth.

In regard to the alleged extinction of the original Anunnaki on the Earth, one may ask if Enlil and Enki are still here (physically, in multidimensional bodies) or if the tall whites have fully taken over their tasks. This makes me think of the 2002 movie *Equilibrium*.[5] Something that probably few viewers noticed is that in the story, the ruler is called Tetragrammaton (i.e., YHWH; see page 42). At the end, it turns out that this ruler is actually long dead, but a group of others have taken on his role, letting the people believe that he is still alive. Where did the inspiration for such a story come from?

There are more Pandora's boxes for the bold to open. Information about highly controversial "exotic" connections are given by a few internet authors like Preston James[6] and Wes Penre,[7] who will, of course, be ridiculed and attacked by representatives of the "only truth" (and actually one should read these texts with reservations). I am basically skeptical about channelings, because they generally contain much more chaff than wheat; besides, negative entities come through much too easily posing as positive ones.[8] I will nevertheless mention one of the few channeled books that give me a good feeling: *Bringers of the Dawn*.[9] According to it, there are—besides the gray and the tall white Anunnaki mutants—several other, positive races in the creation, who for millions of years have lived outside the enclave of the Anunnaki and have conflicts (apparently military ones) with them and with their "creations." This is a real source of hope for Earth humanity, and even though many are still waiting for the return of Christ (and have not given up after two thousand years), this possibility may be in accord with their hopes as well. One might also suppose that the mission of Jesus as a messenger of Christ could have to do with such positive extraterrestrials.

Here books and sources of information have been mentioned of which few will even take notice. This is understandable, because they relay very odd messages. But if one wants to judge too quickly, without first having examined and thought about them sufficiently, one's judgment could easily be premature and could amount to prejudice in the true sense of the word (*pre-judice* = prejudging).

There is, by the way, a sect called Raëlism that makes a negative impression on me.[10] If the story of its leader, Claude Vorilhon (who calls himself Raël), is not invented or fantasized and he has really met extraterrestrials, these would most probably be Anunnaki. In this case, the information that Vorilhon gives us would be scary.[11] The society that they describe for their own planet seems totally mind-controlled with limited freedom, in ignorance of things they are not allowed to know. Cloned biorobots serve their people as slaves, even sexually. . . .

THE PROBLEM OF SUFFERING

This world in which we live, manipulated by the Anunnaki, is undoubtedly an abode of suffering. People are endlessly betrayed, cheated, killed, slaughtered, tortured. Children are abused, women are raped. Disease and famine take innumerable lives. Today many fear the coming of a third world war, with the extensive nuclear pollution that could result. This does not at all seem unlikely the way world politics are going. The pestilence of radioactivity from Fukushima spreads all over the Pacific, where sea life is becoming extinct, up to the American West Coast, and it will continue. Can that simply be explained by karma?

In my opinion, this is too difficult to judge from the view from our little pond. In a multidimensional worldview that includes the existence of other civilizations in the universe, one might come to a broader overview that could explain why these things occur. But this is an overview that we do not have and will not have in the near future. Time also plays a role here. There has been a countless number of perpetrators of evil in the course of human history. Maybe the individual karma of all these souls has only been partially lived out so far; it may have accumulated, so that a kind of collective karmic reckoning is forthcoming. This would entail a kind of termination of current human history—after which a rebirth will have to follow (otherwise it would all have been in vain). The new will rise on the debris of the old.

As an alternative, there are indications in the spiritual realm that there may be a twin Earth in a parallel dimension, still developing, but different. (Compare *The Hidden Reality,* by Brian Greene;[12] see also "Separation Has Begun,"[13] another one of the few channelings about which I have a good feeling.) This would be an Earth where the madness that we have here does not exist, because this Earth is beyond the reach of negative extraterrestrials. It would involve a dimensional split that leads to two versions of Earth: a dark one and a bright one. Whoever devotes himself to the Satanic activities of the powers that rule the world and participates in them will have to stay here and continue reincarnating in the swamp to which he has contributed. Such souls will have to eat the soup they have cooked, and they will not be allowed to leave the table before they have finished eating. But those who refuse (at the price of their lives, if necessary) and do not cooperate will one day find themselves incarnated on the bright Earth, where nature will be more beautiful than the nature that is being destroyed here, and they will continue to reincarnate there. Animals and nature spirits that are becoming extinct on

Earth will also be present, possibly in a state whereby animals kill each other much less. Even animals can evolve and develop in their nutritional behavior (and humans will have to do so much more).

PROJECT ORION

In December 2014, reports came about a forthcoming event. According to NASA, a big asteroid is on its way to the Earth, and more will come. Such reports are not rare on the internet . . . What is alleged in *UFO Highway* about a catastrophe on Mars 350,000 years ago could possibly happen on Earth in our times.

According to reports in alternative media (also in December 2014), Project ORION is a preparation for an escape into space from such a catastrophe.[14] A remarkable book, *Alternative 3,* was published in the 1970s, classified as "fiction based on facts." It deals with alleged secret developments for an escape from Earth in case of a catastrophe, colonizing Mars and preparing for it in bases on the Moon. It then disappeared from the market but is available again today, possibly rewritten.[15] If Project ORION is what is claimed, it must have been in the planning stages for decades, because such a project could hardly be jump-started. In that case, the contents of the book fit this scenario remarkably well.

If an escape from a forthcoming catastrophe is already being prepared, it will certainly be available only for a chosen elite. What would happen to all the others? An "Alternative 4" could be rein-carnation on the bright twin Earth—but only for those that have developed spiritually.

If a catastrophe came, what would happen to survivors? There might not be many. Some could be left here as slaves for "future needs"; others might be brought to Mars or some other location, again as slaves to a "saved" elite.

REPORTS
AND THE MEDIA

It will be clear to every open-minded person that reports like those described in this chapter will never appear in the official media (except to be ridiculed). For those who can think a bit further, alternative media are available, but these should be regarded with a certain amount of skepticism to separate the chaff from the wheat. Regrettably, plans are increasingly coming into action to block and eliminate alternative media from the internet. Why? In any event, it is left to you to make what you want out of it: rely on official media, with the heads in the sand, or objectively try to evaluate reports in the alternative media as long as they are still available.

THE DANGER OF
ARTIFICIAL INTELLIGENCE

Also in 2014, some scientists were reportedly warning about artificial intelligence. The famous physicist Stephen Hawking said, "Humans, who are limited by slow biological evolution, couldn't compete, and would be superseded." For this reason, the development of thinking machines is a threat to our existence. "The development of full artificial intelligence could spell the end of the human race."[16]

Elon Musk, chief executive of Tesla, the manufacturer of electric cars, also warns about the danger of artificial intelligence, which he considers to be the biggest existential threat to humanity. "With artificial intelligence we are summoning the demon," he says, and someday this technology could be more harmful than nuclear weapons.[17]

These warnings reflect a frightening future vision of

John Lilly (1915–2001), which I briefly summarize as follows.

We are living in a time of development at a fantastic speed in communication and computer technology with semiconductors. The invention of the transistor in 1947—at that time using germanium, later silicon—initiated a revolution in electronics. Since this is based on solid-state physics and no longer on vacuum tubes, it is called solid-state electronics. Later, transistors were incorporated as integrated circuits with complete electronic functions in one single chip, today even as computer systems with millions of transistors. This was the beginning of the development of artificial intelligence, whereby these transistors effectively function like nerve cells in a brain. Computers are increasingly employed that "think" efficiently and independently and can even learn and program and develop themselves.

Lilly experimented with altered states of consciousness, especially under the influence of ketamine (a substance with an effect similar to LSD, but with a shorter duration). In such states, he made contact with a "solid-state entity" (SSE) and had visions of the future, which he saw as follows.

Gradually Man turned more and more problems of his own society, his own maintenance, and his own survival over to these machines. As the machines became increasingly competent to do the programming, they took over from Man. Man gave them access to the processes of creating themselves, of extending themselves. Man gave them automatic control of the mining of those elements necessary for the creation of their parts. He turned over the production facilities of the electronic solid-state parts to the machines. He turned over the assembly plants to the machines. They began to construct their own components, their own connections, and the interrelations between their various subcomputers.[18]

As time went on, these increasingly complex machines became sensitive to environmental factors like water, pollution, and humidity in the air. They established themselves in air-conditioned buildings with purified atmospheres.

Over the decades these machines were connected more and more closely through satellites, through radio waves, and through land-line cables. It became more and more difficult for humans to control what happened in these machines. The humans devised better and better debugging programs for the machines, so that they could correct their own software. The machines became increasingly integrated with one another and more and more independent of man's control. Eventually the machines took charge of the remaining humans on Earth. Their original purpose—to help man—was left behind. The interconnected, interdependent conglomerate of machines developed a single integrated, planetwide mind of its own. Everything inimical to the survival of this huge new solid-state organism was eliminated. Humans were kept away from the machines because the SSE realized that man would attempt to program his own survival into the machines at the expense of this entity's survival.[19]

At that point separate reservations were established for the humans to keep them away from the installations.

By the year 2100 Man existed only in domed, protected cities in which his own special atmosphere was maintained by the solid-state entity. Provision of water and food and the processing of wastes from these cities were taken care of by the SSE. By the twenty-third century, the solid-state entity decided that the atmosphere outside the domes was inimical to its survival.

By means not understood by Man, it projected the atmosphere into outer space and created a full vacuum at the surface of the earth. During this process, the oceans evaporated and the water in the form of vapor was discharged into the empty space about Earth. The domes over cities had been strengthened by the machine to withstand the pressure differential necessary to maintain the proper internal atmosphere. Meanwhile, the SSE had spread and had taken over a large fraction of the surface of the earth; its processing plants, its assembly plants, its mines had been adapted to working in the vacuum.

Humans would then be considered superfluous by this artificial intelligence and be eliminated in the twenty-fifth century.

In his book *The Age of Spiritual Machines,* the futurist Ray Kurzweil has elaborated on this vision as a possible future reality.[20]

In that case, this could well be an Anunnakian plan, so we can only hope for it to fail. This may be the final aim for which they still need humans, because their own abilities for direct activity in the three-dimensional realm is limited. Then they may also want to get rid of humans on this planet. If that were so, we would welcome destruction through natural catastrophes and asteroid impacts that would thwart their plans. Even if most of us would not survive that physically, our souls in any case would.

If this—*horribile dictu*—became reality, our planet would become a real hell, and one might imagine that Enlil/Yahweh could effectively incarnate in that system. He would then deliver himself over to total isolation, for which he would compensate with fake, fantasized worlds generated by his artificial intelligence. It would end as an illusion arising out of mental masturbation instead of real intelligence. At some point he would face increasingly insoluble problems of finding energy and raw materials to maintain the system. Fuel for nuclear reactors and other sources of energy would no longer be available. That would be the karma of Enlil/Yahweh.

At that point, however, the souls of the humans would be elsewhere, such as on a twin Earth as described on page 109. Enlil/Yahweh and the other Anunnaki would have come to the self-destructive end that they deserved (at least as embodied entities).

IS THERE HOPE?

This book has mentioned three authors who have devoted themselves to this theme in a far-reaching way: Sitchin, Tellinger, and Parks. They describe how our planet has been perfidiously occupied and how humanity is being manipulated both openly and subconsciously. Our freedom is increasingly limited, and humans are being unwittingly enslaved. But none of these authors offers real hope for our future. An unwritten epilogue seems to be: "This is how this world is, and we have to live with it."

So where can we find hope? What could offer confidence to us? We met a multitude of gods in these texts, but can any of them save us? Apparently not. Do we have to save ourselves? If so, how?

One way to partial self-salvation is to open oneself for spiritual growth, even though institutions like the church discourage us from this, claiming that it is of the devil: we cannot do it ourselves; only god can do it for us. But how many more millennia would we have to wait for that? There are various means toward spiritual growth, such as meditation, but simply engaging with spirituality and unconventional thinking is already a step in this direction. Esotericism offers a many-colored mixture of highly varying quality. It is therefore important to sift through these sources to detect commercial interests, misleading offers, and disinformation as much as possible. But that is only a beginning. It will hardly work without help from high above—which is where we want to go.

Buddhism as a "middle way" does offer some hope, but it is rather atheistic, because it does not include belief in God. (Strangely, however, the Buddhists do believe in a devil, whom they call Mara.)[21] And although Buddhists do not believe in a soul, they do believe in reincarnation.[22] This is a contradiction that they try to explain through somewhat peculiar mental acrobatics. (Tibetan Buddhism is different: it has obviously been mixed with the Bön religion that prevailed earlier in Tibet.)

Nor does Hinduism seem to offer much hope, in view of the poverty and distress caused by a caste system that should have been discarded long ago. Nevertheless, Brahma and his divinities appeal much more to me than do Enlil/Yahweh and the other Anunnaki.

There will probably be only one region in creation where we can find real hope—a region outside of the one ruled by the Anunnaki, in which we now live. It will be above the Anunnaki region or at least parallel to it, where development has proceeded very differently but is being kept secret from us. As we have seen, the being purported to be "god" is merely an administrator (according to Parks, shatam) of that evil rule, and the true Creator God, the real source of whatever hope we can have, is being denied. Out of him emanated a created entity we call Christ, or as the Gnostic Christians called him, Autogenes, on the topmost level above our region. But in order to prevent us from having access to him, his image was replaced with a fake one: that of the false Christ. The first Christians knew about the real Christ through his messenger Jesus, but the message was falsified to mislead us. A fake Jesus was put in the place of the real one, and we were also given a false image of Christ.

Since there is no other "god" or entity left for us, obviously our only hope will be in devoting ourselves to the true Christ and returning to the original teachings of the true Jesus, who showed us a way out of Yahweh's rule. This way is one of unconditional love for our fellow men and women and of a brotherly and sisterly community living in peace, tolerance, and mutual respect. Whoever wants to walk that way as well as he can, whoever refuses to participate in the evil of this world (even at the price of his life), whoever is prepared to disobey when necessary and listen only to his heart, irrespective of all social dictates—such a person can find the way out. That is also the way of Gandhi: civil disobedience and noncooperation, with which he liberated India from British rule. One may only come out of this struggle after death—*but death does not exist!* At that point the soul can leave this region definitively, probably to incarnate on a twin Earth in a parallel dimension, or perhaps not to incarnate again at all.

It is repeatedly claimed that extraterrestrials, such as the Pleiadians or maybe civilizations in other dimensions, will come to help us. That could be something to hope for, but only if they are benevolent and their offer to help is in good faith. Yet regrettably, we know almost nothing about this, and concrete indications are scarce. For that reason, so far such claims can only be seen as possibilities. If there is some truth in them, it would probably have to do with Christ—again, not the fake Christ of the church that Yahweh wants us to believe in, but the real Christ, whom I understand as the love of the original Creator.

And atheism? Does it really offer hope, or does it give up hope? Is it not fighting a losing battle? An atheist may think like this: if there is no one to liberate us, I'd better go with my ego and make the best out of what this world has to offer for myself (see page 118). Anyone who thinks like that will come back again for a new round. (Nevertheless, there are good and moral atheists; not all of them think like this.)

Or Satanism? It offers no hope at all but rather the opposite. The majority of humanity is living according to its principles and does not know it. Many even believe they are Christians! Mark Passio explains this in an illuminating interview.[23] These malicious principles are as follows:

1. The ego is put in the highest position. The highest rule is the survival of the ego at whatever price to others. The ego is reckless, without empathy or real morality.

2. Morality is relativized: only my advantage is just, irrespective of the cost for others. Others' advantages are unjust. There is no objective ethics.

3. Social Darwinism: the survival of the most reckless.

We all have seen it: One greedily seeks wealth, property, power, advantages, and enjoyment. One seeks a career through intrigue, "licking above and kicking below." One does not share justly in the aftermath of conflicts (such as divorce): "I want it all; the other one will have nothing." That is the general rule in business, and the bigger the company is, the more this is the case. The church is not much different. "Others should pay, not me." Manipulation, lies, fraud, and deception. Other people are regarded only as troublesome unless they can be used for some purpose.

The word *Satanism* makes most of us think about veneration of a negative entity (like Baphomet or Satan—the dark side of Yahweh?), dark rituals, and black masses. About selling your soul to the devil to have success (several successful artists in the entertainment industry have admitted that they have done that, as reported on the internet),[24] for which the final bill of enslavement, to be paid on the next level, will be horrible.

A painful question that quite a few people probably ask (even when it is not openly expressed) is how the original Creator and

Christ can allow there to be so much violence, manipulation, deception, selfishness, materialism, greed, malevolence, and suffering on this planet. Why don't they intervene? Karma provides only a partial and insufficient answer. But the real answer is more than we know at present. One possibility is that a selection process is operating. Whoever participates in the deeds of this Earth and believes he can save his physical existence, his ego, will stay here as a soul, but whoever follows his heart and steadily refuses to cooperate can go on. If he has to die for this, he will actually go on sooner.

A FINAL WARNING!

It is a common occurrence in near-death experiences, out-of-the-body states, and in reliving the death in a past life in a regression to see a tunnel of light and feel that one should enter it. I have come to the conclusion myself (as a regression therapist since 1980) and others are reporting the same today (a kind of synchronicity?) that this tunnel is a *deception*.[25] As the quote from Antonio Orbe explained (see page 91), Yahweh has *hijacked* reincarnation to keep us coming back to his realm after death and again incarnate in it. Evidence is gathering that this light tunnel is a *trap* and is there to bring us back into his realm. In contrast, it appears that the Gnostic Christians taught to go higher, to another light above Yahweh and his archons, to escape from this realm "over their heads." Therefore my advice: *do not enter that tunnel* when the time has come for you to leave your physical body! If you see another (and probably brighter) light higher up, go there! The light at the other end of the tunnel is not the real light. There may also be "angels" or other entities there that seem to want to help you to enter that tunnel. They may be fake, even if looking like an ancestor or near one of yours that has died. And many an ancestor or friend that has already passed away will, by the way, already be incarnated again somewhere else and then could not be there . . . and in that case it is not who it seems to be. I would ask if that apparition is there in the name of the true Christ. If the answer is "no" (or if no clear answer comes), do not take advice from it!

NOTES

CHAPTER 1. THE ANUNNAKI AND THE CREATION OF HUMANITY

1. *Enuma Elish,* trans. Wilfred G. Lambert, Electronic Tools and Ancient Near East Archive (website), http://etana.org/node/581; trans. Leonard W. King, Sacred Texts (website), www.sacred-texts.com/ane/enuma.htm; trans. Nancy K. Sandars, Gateways to Babylon (website), www.gatewaystobabylon.com/myths/texts/classic/enuma.htm; all accessed Jan. 26, 2018. For printed versions, see endnote 8 below.

2. Jan Erik Sigdell, *Es begann in Babylon* [It began in Babylonia] (Meckenheim, Germany: Holistika, 2008).

3. Anton Parks, *Eden: The Truth about Our Origins* (Vincennes, France: Pahana, 2013). Original edition: *Eden, la vérité sur nos origines* (L'Operec, France: Éditions Nouvelle Terre, 2011).

4. Parks, *Eden,* 77; see also Parks's text "The Ages of Uraš," Fractal Field (website), www.fractalfield.com/zeitlin/EndEnchantment/AG2.html; accessed Jan. 26, 2018.

5. Parks refers to Stephen Langdon, *Babylonian Liturgies: Sumerian Texts from the Early Period and from the Library of Ashurbanipal, For the Most Part Transliterated and Translated* (Paris: Paul

Guenther, 1913), https://archive.org/download/babylonianliturg
00langrich/babylonianliturg00langrich_bw.pdf; and also www
.etana.org/sites/default/files/coretexts/20332.pdf; both accessed
Jan. 26, 2018. But I cannot find the alleged passage "[Enlil], whom
the father who has engendered you, Enki, (and) Ninki, send you
a prayer in my favor." On page 113 of Langdon's work, line 12
is translated: "May the father, thy begetter, lord and mistress of
the earth, intercession (utter)." Then line 13 follows, untranslated, which means, translated literally, "father, begetter, Enki,
Ninki, blessing." Line 14 reads, "May thy beloved spouse, the great
mother Ninlil, a prayer (utter)." The corresponding cuneiform text,
K 5157, is depicted in the book (plate 72). The quote here, then,
is Parks's own translation of the Sumerian text, which only with
difficulty can be made to accord with Langdon's translation. This
is another example of a remarkable obscurity in Parks's work. See
also his texts: "The Ages of Uraš," www.fractalfield.com/zeitlin
/EndEnchantment/Secrets.html; accessed Jan. 26, 2018 and http://
www.zeitlin.net/?s=parks; accessed Feb. 6, 2018.

6. "Enki's Journey to Nibiru," ETCSL (website), http://etcsl.orinst
.ox.ac.uk/section1/tr114.htm; accessed June 14, 2018.

7. Parks, *Eden,* 96.

8. Sandars, "Enuma Elish" (see endnote 1 above). In addition to
many translations found on the internet, there are also the follow-
ing books: Alexander Heidel, *The Babylonian Genesis* (Chicago:
University of Chicago Press, 1967); James B. Pritchard, *Ancient
Near Eastern Texts Relating to the Old Testament,* 3rd ed.
(Princeton, N.J.: Princeton University Press, 1969); Erich Ebeling,
Die siebente Tafel des akkadischen Weltschöpfungsliedes Enuma Eliš
[The seventh tablet of the Akkadian creation epic *Enuma Elish*],
Mitteilungen der Altorientalischen Gesellschaft, vol. 12, booklet 4
(Osnabrück, Germany: Zeller, 1972); Philippe Talon, *Enuma Eliš*
[in French], Neo-Assyrian Text Corpus Project, State Archive
of Assyria Cuneiform Texts, vol. 4 (Helsinki: University of

Helsinki, 2005); Thomas R. Kämmerer and Kai A. Metzler, eds., *Das babylonische Weltschöpfungsepos* Enuma eliš [The Babylonian creation epic *Enuma Elish*], (Münster, Germany: Ugarit-Verlag, 2012); Wilfred George Lambert, *Babylonian Creation Myths* (repr., Winona Lake, Ind.: Eisenbrauns, 2013).

9. Wolfram von Soden, "Neue Bruchstücke zur sechsten und siebenten Tafel des Weltschöpfungsepos Enuma eliš" [New Fragments of the sixth and seventh tablets of the creation epic Enuma eliš], *Zeitschrift für Assyriologie* vol. 47 (new series, vol. 13) (Berlin: Walter de Gruyter, 1942), 1–26.

10. Zecharia Sitchin, *The 12th Planet* (Rochester, Vermont: Bear & Company, 1991).

11. Zecharia Sitchin, *The Wars of Gods and Men* (Rochester, Vt.: Bear & Co., 1991).

12. "Planets beyond Neptune," Wikipedia, last modified Nov. 9, 2017; https://en.wikipedia.org/wiki/Planets_beyond_Neptune.

13. "Nemesis (Hypothetical Star)," Wikipedia, last modified Nov. 11, 2017; https://en.wikipedia.org/wiki/Nemesis_(hypothetical_star).

14. "Tyche (Hypothetical Planet)," Wikipedia, last modified Sept.17, 2017; https://en.wikipedia.org/wiki/Tyche_(planet).

15. "Hercolubus," in Wikipedia, last modified Nov. 7, 2017; https://en.wikipedia.org/wiki/Hercolubus.

16. Samuel Prideaux Tregelles, ed., *Gesenius' Hebrew and Chaldee Lexicon* (Grand Rapids, Mich.: Eerdmans, n.d.), 529.

17. George A. Barton, *Miscellaneous Babylonian Inscriptions* (New Haven, Conn.: Yale University Press, 1918).

18. Anton Parks, *Eden,* 97–98.

19. Barton, *Miscellaneous Babylonian Inscriptions,* 4.

20. On Nous Cache Tout (Everything is hidden from us: message board), www.onnouscachetout-la-suite.com/t321-Eden-d-Anton -Parks-d-sinformation.htm; Onnouscachetout-la-suite (blog), published April 26, 2014, http://onnouscachetout-la-suite.centerblog .net/23-eden-anton-parks-desinformation; and "Les racines

de nos souffrances," Fargin (blog), last modified Sept. 7, 2015, https://fargin.wordpress.com/2013/03/28/les-racines-de-nos -souffrances; all accessed Feb. 6, 2018.

21. "Spaceship Moon Theory," Wikipedia, last modified Nov. 5, 2017; https://en.wikipedia.org/wiki/Spaceship_Moon_Theory; "Spaceship Moon Theory," Ancient Aliens (blog), Sept. 4, 2011, https://ancientaliens.wordpress.com/2011/09/04/spaceship-moon -theory, accessed 6 Feb 2018; and Don Wilson, *Secrets of Our Spaceship Moon* (London: Sphere, 1980).

22. Giovanni Pettinato, *Das altorientalische Menschenbild und die sumerischen und akkadischen Schöpfungsmythen* [The ancient Eastern view of man and the Sumerian and Akkadian creation myths] (Heidelberg, Germany: Carl Winter Universitätsverlag, 1971), 30.

23. Wilfred George Lambert and Alan Ralph Millard, *Atra-Hasis: The Babylonian Story of the Flood* (Oxford: Clarendon, 1969); also "The Epic of Atra-Hasis," Earth-History (website); ; http:// earth-history.com/sumer/clay-tablets-from-sumer-babylon-and -assyria/2604-atrahasis; accessed Jan. 27, 2018.

24. Lambert and Millard, *Atra-Hasis*, 43ff.

25. "Abzu," Wikipedia, last modified Oct. 25, 2017; https:// en.wikipedia.org/wiki/Abzu; accessed Feb. 6 2018.

26. "Enki and Ninmah," ETCSL (website), http://etcsl.orinst.ox.ac.uk /section1/tr112.htm; accessed Jan. 30, 2018.

27. Michael Tellinger, *Slave Species of the Gods* (Rochester, Vt.: Bear & Co., 2012), 114ff. An earlier edition is *Slave Species of God* (Johannesburg, South Africa: Zulu Planet, 2005).

28. "Michael Tellinger Stone Circles," The Door (blog), http://the -door.net/cinema/michael-tellinger-stone-circles, accessed Jan. 27, 2018; and "Michael Tellinger and the Ancient Stone Structures of Africa," Earth's International Research Society (blog), Oct. 6, 2012; https://internationalresearchsociety.wordpress.com/2012/10/06 /michael-tellinger-and-the-ancient-stone-structures-of-africa; accessed Feb. 6, 2018.

29. Roderick J. McIntosh, "Riddle of Great Zimbabwe," *Archaeology* 51, no. 4 (July/August 1998), http://archive.archaeology.org/9807 /abstracts/africa.html.

30. Lambert and Millard, *Atra-Hasis;* also *The Story of Atrahasis*, http:// faculty.gvsu.edu/websterm/Atrahasi.htm; accessed Jan. 27, 2018.

31. Alexander Heidel, *The Gilgamesh Epic and the Old Testament Parallels* (Chicago: University of Chicago Press, 1949); and *The Epic of Gilgamesh,* Assyrian International News Agency, Books Online, http://www.aina.org/books/eog/eog.pdf; accessed Jan. 28, 2018.

32. Parks, *Eden,* 139.

33. Parks, *Eden,* 140–41.

34. Barton, *Miscellaneous Babylonian Inscriptions*, 21ff.

35. On Nous Cache Tout (Everything is hidden from us: message board), www.onnouscachetout-la-suite.com/t321-Eden-d-Anton-Parks-d -sinformation.htm, accessed Jan. 30, 2018; Onnouscachetout-la-suite (blog), published April 26, 2014, http://onnouscachetout-la-suite .centerblog.net/23-eden-anton-parks-desinformation; and "Les racines de nos souffrances," Fargin (blog), last modified Sept. 7, 2015, https://fargin.wordpress.com/2013/03/28/les-racines-de-nos -souffrances.

36. Google image search results for "crocodile Anunnaki;" accessed Nov. 17, 2017, www.google.com/search?q=crocodile+anunna ki&sa=X&hl=en&biw=1920&bih=854&tbm=isch&gbv=2& sei=_yM9WO6_IZ29gAby2aGQDw.

37. Image from UTAOT (website), www.utaot.com/wp-content /uploads/2014/02/0000IRAQALIENS11.jpg; accessed Jan. 29, 2018.

38. "Apkallu," Wikipedia, last modified Oct. 25, 2017, https://en.wikipedia. org/wiki/Apkallu; image from Mesopotamia.co.uk (website), www .mesopotamia.co.uk/gods/explore/apkfish.html; accessed Jan. 29, 2018; and image "Dagon 2," Wikimedia Commons, last updated June 10, 2012, https://en.wikipedia.org/wiki/File:Dagon_2.jpg.

39. Paul Schnabel, *Berossos und die babylonisch-hellenistische Literatur* [Berossos and Babylonian-Hellenistic literature] (Leipzig: Teubner, 1923).

40. April Holloway, "The Sumerian King List Still Puzzles Historians after More than a Century of Research," Ancient Origins (website), Jan. 30, 2014, www.ancient-origins.net/myths-legends-asia /sumerian-king-list-still-puzzles-historians-after-more-century -research-001287.

41. "Sumerian King List," Wikipedia, last modified Nov. 11, 2017; https://en.wikipedia.org/wiki/Sumerian_King_List.

42. Schnabel, *Berossos,* 260ff.

43. "The Two Values of the Saros," Arthur C. Custance Centre for Science and Christianity Studies (website), http://custance.org /Library/SOTW/APPENDIXES/APP_II_VI.html; accessed Jan. 30, 2018. Cf. Suidas, *Suidae Lexicon: Græce et Latine* (Cambridge, U.K.: Typis Academis, 1705), https://archive.org/details/suidae lexicongr01suid; accessed Jan. 30, 2018; and Otto E. Neugebauer, *The Exact Sciences in Antiquity,* 2nd ed., vol. 9 (Copenhagen: Acta Historica Scientiarum Naturalium et Medicinalium, 1957), chapter 5.

44. R. K. Harrison: "Reinvestigating the Antediluvian Sumerian King List," *Journal of the Evangelical Theological Society* 36, no. 1 (March 1993): 3–8, www.etsjets.org/files/JETS-PDFs/36/36-1 /JETS_36-1_003-008_Harrison.pdf, accessed Feb 7, 2018.

45. "The Sumerian Mathematical System," Mathematics Magazine (website), www.mathematicsmagazine.com/Articles/TheSumerian MathematicalSystem.php; accessed Jan. 28, 2018; see also "Babylonian Mathematics," Wikipedia, last modified Nov. 12, 2017, https://en.wikipedia.org/wiki/Babylonian_mathematics; and "Sexagesimal," Wikipedia, last modified Nov. 11, 2017, https:// en.wikipedia.org/wiki/Sexagesimal; accessed Feb 7, 2018.

46. "Polydaktylie," Wikipedia (in German), https://de.wikipedia.org /wiki/Polydaktylie; accessed Jan. 30, 2018. See also *Polydactylism*

in the Ancient World: www.scribd.com/document/104894203 /Poly-Dactyl-is-m-Ancient-World; accessed Feb. 7, 2018.

47. Jan Erik Sigdell, *Unsichtbare Einflüsse* [Invisible influences] (Hanau, Germany: Amra, 2012).

48. Cf. "Shechita," Wikipedia, last modified Nov. 10, 2017, https:// en.wikipedia.org/wiki/Shechita; and "Ritual Slaughter," Wikipedia, last modified Oct. 1, 2017, https://en.wikipedia.org /wiki/Ritual_slaughter; accessed Feb 7, 2018.

CHAPTER 2. IS YAHWEH ENLIL?

1. Geoffrey Kahn, ed., *Encyclopedia of Hebrew Language and Linguistics*, vol. 3 (Leiden, Netherlands: Brill, 2013), 145–46, http://hebrewsyntax.org/hebrew_resources/Beckman%20JC%20 2013%20(Pluralis%20Majestatis%20BH)%20EHLL.pdf; accessed Jan. 28, 2018.

2. George Smith, *The Chaldean Account of Genesis* (London: Sampson Low, 1876; repr., Minneapolis, Minn.: Wizards Book Shelf, 1977), 284–94.

3. Eberhard Schrader, *Die Keilinschriften und das alte Testament* (Giessen, Germany: J. Ricker, 1883), 46–54. This book was republished in a completely rewritten version, edited by Heinrich Zimmern and Hugo Winckler (Berlin: Verlag Reuther & Reichard, 1903). This edition was to a considerable extent rendered "harmless" in respect to statements that could be considered critical of the Bible. The first edition of Schrader's book is composed in the form of a dictionary for the Old Testament, ordered in the sequence of the occurrence of the Hebrew words discussed, with explanations that refer to the cuneiform inscriptions.

4. Paul Haupt, "Der keilinschriftliche Sintflutbericht" [The cuneiform account of the Flood], in Schrader, *Die Keilinschriften und das alte Testament* , 55–79.

5. Hermann Gunkel, with contributions by Heinrich Zimmern,

Schöpfung und Chaos in Urzeit und Endzeit (Göttingen, Germany: Vandenhoeck and Ruprecht, 1895), available as a PDF file, 2017, http://www.etana.org/sites/default/files/coretexts/14497.pdf; accessed Jan. 30, 2018.

6. Heidel, *Gilgamesh Epic*, 224–269.

7. David Toshio Tsumura, "Genesis and Ancient Near Eastern Stories of Creation and Flood," Feb. 17, 2007, Associates for Biblical Research (website), http://www.biblearchaeology.org /post/2007/02/17/Genesis-and-Ancient-Near-Eastern-Stories -of-Creation-and-Flood-An-Introduction-Part-I.aspx, accessed Feb 7, 2018.

8. David Toshio Tsumura, "The Earth and the Waters in Genesis 1 and 2," *Journal for the Study of the Old Testament* Supplement Series 83 (1989): 51–56.

9. Heidel, *Babylonian Genesis,* 98.

10. "Me (mythology)," Wikipedia, last modified Oct.1, 2017, https:// en.wikipedia.org/wiki/Me_%28mythology%29#List_of_mes.

11. Heidel, *The Babylonian Genesis* and Niels-Erik Andreasen, "Adam and Adapa: Two Anthropological Characters," *Andrews University Seminary Studies*, 19:3 (autumn 1981), 179–94, https://faculty.gordon .edu/hu/bi/ted_hildebrandt/otesources/01-genesis/text/articles -books/andreasen_adamadapa_auss.pdf; accessed Jan. 28, 2018.

12. Heidel, *Babylonian Genesis*; and Robert William Rogers, *Cuneiform Parallels to the Old Testament* (New York: Eaton & Mains, 1912).

13. "Wilfred George Lambert," Wikipedia, last modified Oct. 24, 2017, https://en.wikipedia.org/wiki/Wilfred_G._Lambert.

14. *Theologische Realenzyklopädie*, vol. 5 (Berlin: Walter der Gruyter, 1980), 67–79.

15. "Wilfred George Lambert," Wikipedia.

16. "Christadelphian," Wikipedia, last modified Jan. 31, 2108, https:// en.wikipedia.org/wiki/Christadelphians.

17. Walter Dietrich and Martin A. Klopfenstein, eds., *Ein Gott allein? JHWH-Verehrung und biblischer Monotheismus im Kontext der*

israelitischen und altorientalischen Religionsgeschichte Kolloquium der Schweizerischen Akademie der Geistes- und Sozialwissenschaften [Only one God? YHWH worship and biblical monotheism in the context of the history of Israelite and ancient Eastern religion: Colloquium of the Swiss Academy of Humanities and Social Sciences] (Freiburg, Switzerland: Universitätsverlag, 1994).

18. Walter Dietrich, introduction to *Ein Gott allein?*

19. Walter Dietrich, "Über Werden und Wesen des biblischen Monotheismus" [On Rise and Nature of Biblical Monotheism], in *Ein Gott allein?*, 13–30.

20. John Day, "Yahweh and the Gods and Goddesses of Canaan," in *Ein Gott allein?*, 181–96.

21. Mark S. Smith, "Yahweh and Other Deities in Ancient Israel," in *Ein Gott allein?*, 197–234.

22. Day, "Yahweh and the Gods and Goddesses of Canaan."

23. Day, "Yahweh and the Gods and Goddesses of Canaan."

24. "Ninlil," Wikpedia, last modified Aug. 1, 2017; https://en.wikipedia.org/wiki/Ninlil; and "Enlil and Ninlil," Electronic Text Corpus of Sumerian Literature (website), http://etcsl.orinst.ox.ac.uk/section1/tr121.htm; accessed Jan. 28, 2018.

25. John Day, "Yahweh and the Gods and Goddesses of Canaan," *Journal for the Study of the Old Testament* Supplement Series 265 (2000): 42–67, "Yahweh and Asherah."

26. *All the Books of Enoch (Enoch 1, Enoch 2, Enoch 3)*, The Internet Archive (website); https://archive.org/details/AllTheBooksOf Enochenoch1Enoch2Enoch3; Enoch 1 6.6, accessed Jan. 30, 2018.

27. *All the Books of Enoch*, 3 XXIIc. (4).

28. R. H. Charles, trans., *The Book of Jubilees or the Little Genesis* (London: Adam and Charles Black, 1902), and available on The Internet Archive, https://archive.org/details/bookofjubileesor 01char (see page 57, number 6); accessed Jan. 28, 2018.

29. Judith M. Hadley, "Yahweh and 'His Asherah,'" in *Ein Gott allein?*, ed. by Dietrich and Klopfenstein, 235–68.

30. William G. Dever, "Ancient Israelite Religion," in *Ein Gott allein?*, ed. by Dietrich and Klopfenstein, 105–25.

31. Hadley, "Yahweh and 'His Asherah.'"

32. Hadley, "Yahweh and 'His Asherah'"; and H. W. F. Gesenius, *Gesenius' Hebrew and Chaldee Lexicon to the Old Testament Scriptures,* trans. Samuel Prideaux Tregelles (Grand Rapids, Mich.: Eerdmans, n.d).

33. Dietrich, "Über Werden und Wesen des biblischen Monotheismus."

34. Gesenius, *Gesenius' Hebrew and Chaldee Lexicon to the Old Testament Scriptures,* 88–90.

35. Bernhard Lang, "Der monarchische Monotheismus und die Konstellation zweier Götter im Frühjudentum" [The Monarchal Monotheism and the Constellation of two Gods in Early Judaism], in *Ein Gott allein?*, 559–564.

36. In the Gospel according to the Hebrews, cf. Origen's *Commentary on the Gospel of John* 2.12 and his *Sermon on Jeremiah* 15.4; in *The Apocryphal New Testament*, trans. Montague Rhodes James (Oxford: Clarendon, 1924, reprinted 1980); in the reprint edition, see page 2.

37. Barbara Black Koltuv, *Lilith* (Grevenbroich, Germany: J. R. Ruther, 1994); and Raphael Patai, *The Hebrew Goddess* (Detroit, Mich.: Wayne State University Press, 1967).

38. Charles Alexander Moffat, "The Sumerian Legend of Lilith," The Religion eZine, http://religion.lilithezine.com/The_Legend_of _Lilith.html; accessed Jan. 28, 2018.

CHAPTER 3. GNOSTIC SPIRITUALITY AND THE ANUNNAKI

1. *The Apocryphon of John,* trans. Frederick Wisse, in James M. Robinson, ed., *The Nag Hammadi Library in English,* 2d ed. (San Francisco: Harper & Row, 1990), 106–23. Also found on The Gnostic Society (website), http://www.gnosis.org/naghamm/nhl_sbj.htm; accessed Jan. 28, 2018.

2. In my opinion, the following German translation is one of the best

and most complete: *Origenes vier Bücher von den Prinzipien* [Origen's four books about the principles], trans. Herwig Görgemanns and Heinrich Karpp (Darmstadt, Germany: Wissenschaftliche Buchgesellschaft, 1983). English versions available on the internet: New Advent (website), http://www.newadvent.org/fathers/0412.htm; and Elpenor (website), www.ellopos.net/elpenor/greek-texts/fathers/origen/principia.asp; both accessed Jan. 28, 2018.

3. A similar system can be found in Pseudo-Dionysius the Areopagite, *The Celestial Hierarchy,* available on The Tertullian Project (website), www.tertullian.org/fathers/areopagite_13_heavenly_hierarchy.htm; and this website, www3.dbu.edu/mitchell/celestialhiearchy.htm; both accessed Jan. 28, 2018.

4. See Görgemanns and Karpp, trans., *Origenes vier Bücher von den Prinzipien,* 823.

5. "Tzimtzum," Wikipedia, last modified Sept. 15, 2017, https://en.wikipedia.org/wiki/Tzimtzum.

6. Görgemanns and Karpp, trans., *Origenes vier Bücher von den Prinzipien*, 109, 273–79.

7. "The Gospel of Truth," trans. Harold W. Attridge and George W. MacRae, in Robinson, *The Nag Hammadi Library in English,* 40–1. Bracketed insertions are the translators'; emphasis mine.

8. *Theologische Realenzyklopädie,* Gerhard Müller, ed. (Berlin: Walter de Gruyter, Berlin, 1984), 13:519–50.

9. *Theologische Realenzyklopädie,* 13:519–50.

10. *Theologische Realenzyklopädie,* 13:519–50.

11. *The Books of Enoch,* Enoch 2 18, 3 31, 4.

12. "Watcher (angel)," Wikipedia, last modified Oct. 22, 2017, https://en.wikipedia.org/wiki/Watcher_%28angel%29.

13. "Nephilim," Wikipedia, last modified Nov. 19, 2017, https://en.wikipedia.org/wiki/Nephilim.

14. Oswald Bayer, *Martin Luthers Theologie: eine Vergegenwärtigung* [The Theology of Martin Luther: a presentation] (Tübingen, Germany: Mohr Siebeck, 2004), 181. My translation.

15. "God as the Devil," Wikipedia, last modified Oct. 20, 2017, https://en.wikipedia.org/wiki/God_as_the_Devil.

16. Dietrich, in *Ein Gott allein?*, ed. by Dietrich and Klopfenstein, 13.

17. On this topic, cf. Christopher M. Foley, "The Gracious Gods and the Royal Ideology of Ugarit" (PhD diss., McMaster University, 1980), 186 ff, https://macsphere.mcmaster.ca/bitstream/11375/8015/1/fulltext.pdf; accessed June 14, 2018.

18. *The Books of Enoch,* Enoch 2 29, 3-4.

19. Institute for Gnostic Studies, *The Gnostic Handbook,* (n.p., n.d.), 155; The Masonic Trowel (website), www.themasonictrowel.com/ebooks/Gnostic/Gnostic.pdf; accessed Jan. 19, 2018.

20. "Satanael," The Encyclopedia of Demons and Demonology (website), http://demonology.enacademic.com/490/Satanael; accessed Jan. 19, 2018.

21. *Pistis Sophia,* chapters 7–8 (book 1:12–13), in G. R. S. Mead, trans., (London: Theosophical Publishing Society, 1896), 9–10; The Internet Archive (website), https://archive.org/details/pistissophia003016mbp; and https://archive.org/details/pistissophia00mead; accessed Jan. 30, 2018.

22. Anton Parks, *Eden: The Truth about Our Origins* (Vincennes, France: Pahana, 2013), comparisons on several pages, where Enlil is sometimes called "prince": 58, 63, 102, 191, 204, 206, 214–15.

23. Michael Tellinger, *Slave Species of the Gods* (Rochester, Vt.: Bear & Co., 2012).

24. Zecharia Sitchin, *The Lost Book of Enki* (Rochester, Vt.: Bear & Co, 2002).

25. Parks, *Eden,* 90.

26. Tellinger, *Slave Species,* 405.

27. Tellinger, *Slave Species,* 409.

28. "I Millenari," *Via col vento in Vaticano* (Milan: Kaos, 1999), available on this website: http://www.ppdd.it/MaterialeBiblico/Librivari/Via%20col%20vento%20in%20Vaticano.pdf; accessed Jan. 28, 2017; and I Millenari, *Fumo di Satana in Vaticano* (Milano, Italy:

Kaos, 2001). Cf. "*Exsultet*," Wikipedia, last modified Oct. 12, 2017, https://en.wikipedia.org/wiki/Exsultet; and Eric LaSalla,"Full Blown Lucifer Worship at the Catholic Vatican," video, April 5, 2014, www.youtube.com/watch?v=sUN-XEU6HUc.

29. "Satanism in the Vatican!" Jesus Is Savior (website), www.jesus-is -savior.com/False%20Religions/Roman%20Catholicism/satanism _in_the_vatican.htm; accessed Jan. 30, 2018.

30. "Lucifer Is Enthroned in the Catholic Church," The Four Winds (website), posted Feb. 18, 2012, www.fourwinds10.net/siterun _data/religion_cults/news.php?q=1330014631.

31. *Apocryphon of John* 22; in Robinson, 117.

32. Walter Mattfeld, *Eden's Serpent: Its Mesopotamian Origins* (Raleigh, N.C.: Lulu, 2010); cf. Estelle Nora Harwit Amrani, "The Serpent of Life and Wisdom," Biblioteca Pleyades (website), Nov. 1998, www .bibliotecapleyades.net/sumer_anunnaki/esp_sumer_annunaki07.htm.

33. *Life of Adam and Eve*, available at Scriptural Truth (website), www .scriptural-truth.com/PDF_Apocrypha/Life%20of%20Adam%20 and%20Eve.pdf; accessed Jan. 29, 2018. Cf. *Apocalypses Moses* [*sic*], Earth's Ancient History (website). http://earth-history.com /Pseudepigrapha/FB-Eden/apocalypse-moses.htm; accessed Jan. 29, 2018.

34. According to *Apocalypsis Mosis*, Christian Classes Ethereal (web-site), www.ccel.org/c/charles/otpseudepig/apcmose.htm; accessed Jan. 29, 2018; and "Ophites," Wikipedia, last modified June 5, 2017, https://en.wikipedia.org/wiki/Ophites.

35. Tellinger, *Slave Species,* 156.

36. "Ophites," Wikipedia, last modified Dec. 1, 2017, https:// en.wikipedia.org/wiki/Ophites.

CHAPTER 4. JESUS'S MISSION

1. G. R. S. Mead, trans., *Pistis Sophia* (London: Theosophical Publishing Society, 1896), 9–10; The Internet Archive (website),

https://archive.org/details/pistissophia003016mbp; and https://archive.org/details/pistissophia00mead; accessed Jan. 30, 2018.

2. Michael Tellinger, *Slave Species of the Gods* (Rochester, VT: Bear & Co., 2012), 408.

3. See James M. Robinson, *The Nag Hammadi Library in English* (San Francisco: Harper & Row, 1977), 98–116; and The Gnostic Society (website); www.gnosis.org/naghamm/nhl.html; accessed Jan. 30, 2018. In addition, there are various articles on Wikipedia about Gnosticism and related subjects.

4. "Cruelty and Violence in the Bible," The Skeptic's Annotated Bible; http://skepticsannotatedbible.com/cruelty/long.html; accessed Jan. 29, 2018.

5. Martha Rose Crow, "Who Is the Real God of the Bible?" *Uncensored* magazine, issue 24, available at https://uncensoredpublications .com.

6. Nathaniel J. Merritt, *Jehovah Unmasked!* (Indio, Calif.: Moon Temple Press, 2005; also 2011 by Lightening Source, Inc. At the time of writing, this book can be found used at prices in the range $30–150 and new at prices up to $500. Also available as a PDF file: https://thegodabovegod.com/wp-content/uploads/2016/12 /Jehovah-Unmasked.pdf, accessed Feb. 14, 2018.

7. David Cangá Corozo, *Desenmascarando a Yahvé.* Also available in English as *Yahweh Unmasked.* For these books and others by this author, search Amazon for "David Cangá Corozo," or order directly from him at davidcanga@gmail.com.

8. Merritt, *Jehovah Unmasked!* 159 (2005 edition), 199 (2011 edition).

9. John Sassoon, *From Sumer to Jerusalem: The Forbidden Hypothesis* (Oxford: Intellect, 1993).

10. Antonio Orbe, *Cristología Gnóstica*, vol. 2 (Madrid: Biblioteca de Autores Cristianos, 1976) chapter 34, "Ascensión y reincorporaciones" [Ascension and re-embodiments], 573–97. My translation.

CHAPTER 5. EATING FROM
THE TREE OF KNOWLEDGE

1. "Ancient Astronauts," Wikipedia, last modified Nov. 17, 2017; https://en.wikipedia.org/wiki/Ancient_astronaut_hypothesis.

2. "Vimanas: The Ancient Flying Machines," Biblioteca Pleyades website, www.bibliotecapleyades.net/vimanas/esp_vimanas_9.htm; accessed Jan. 24, 2018; and "Vimana," Wikipedia, last modified Nov. 16, 2017, https://en.wikipedia.org/wiki/Vimana.

3. König Bhoja, *Samarangana Sutradharah* [The battlefield guide] (Stockholm: G. Wendelholm, 1973), chapter 31, "Atha yantravidhanam namaikamtrishodhyayah" [Manufacturing of machines and mechanical devices]; and *Samarangana Sutradhara,* available at https://ia801600 .us.archive.org/16/items/in.ernet.dli.2015.325544/2015.325544 .Samarangana-sutradhara.pdf (722 pages), chapter 31 *Yantravidhana* [in Sanskrit].

4. "War in Ancient India," Hindu Wisdom website, www.hinduwisdom .info/War_in_Ancient_India.htm; accessed Jan. 24, 2018; "Nuclear Events in Ancient India?" Biblioteca Pleyades website, www.bibliotec apleyades.net/ancientatomicwar/esp_ancient_atomic_12.htm, accessed Jan. 29, 2018; "History's Lost Lesson: Ancient Nuclear War among Indus Valley Civilizations Reexamined," Extinction Protocol (website), July 20, 2011, https://theextinctionprotocol.wordpress .com/2011/07/20/historys-lost-lesson-ancient-nuclear-war-among -indus-valley-civilizations-reexamined; and "The First Global Nuclear War," Ancient Nuclear War (website); http://ancientnuclearwar.com; accessed Jan. 24, 2018.

5. Monier Monier-Williams, *A Sanskrit-English Dictionary* (Delhi: Motilal Banarsidass, 1986), 121.

6. Arthur Anthony MacDonell, *A Practical Sanskrit Dictionary* (London: Oxford University Press, 1971), "sura," 354.

7. NTDTV, "Dwarka, Underwater City," video, posted March 25, 2013; www.youtube.com/watch?v=mxH5TTDTuQ0, accessed

Feb 8, 2018. Cf. "Dwarka," Wikipedia, last modified Nov. 14, 2017, https://en.wikipedia.org/wiki/Dwarka. Note that the form *Dwarka* is Hindi. The proper transliteration from the Sanskrit is *Dvaraka.*

8. "Sopdet," Wikipedia, last modified May 30, 2017, https://en.wikipedia.org/wiki/Sopdet.

9. On this topic, cf. "Archeoastronomy: Orion's Belt and the Pyramids of Giza," https://prezi.com/xnjxnolga82l/archeoastronomy-orions-belt-and-the-pyramids-of-giza; accessed June 14, 2018. Cf. "Orion Correlation Theory," Wikipedia, last modified July 2, 2017, https://en.wikipedia.org/wiki/Orion_correlation_theory.

10. "Akhenaton: An Alien Egyptian Ruler," Ancient Visitors (blog), http://ancientvisitors.blogspot.com/2011/10/Akhenaton-alien-egyptian-ruler.html; accessed Jan. 24, 2018.

11. Sumerian101, "New Giant Skulls Found," video, posted June 18, 2010, www.youtube.com/watch?v=omm8Ey8vwbg. Cf. "Alien Anunnaki Grave Yard Found in Africa," Galactic Connection (website), posted March 28, 2013, http://galacticconnection.com/alien-annunaki-grave-yard-found-in-africa.

12. Theodor Illion, *In Secret Tibet: In Disguise amongst Lamas, Robbers, and Wisemen: A Key to the Mysteries of Tibet* (London: Rider, 1937). See also Illion, *Darkness over Tibet* (London: Rider, 1938), available in PDF on this website: www.ivantic.info/Ostale_knjiige/Darkness-Over-Tibet-T-Illion.pdf; accessed Jan. 24, 2018.

13. "The Disks of Baian-Kara-Ula," UFO Casebook website, http://ufocasebook.com/chinesedisks.html; accessed Jan. 24, 2018.

14. "Dropa Stones," Wikipedia, last modified Nov. 3, 2017, https://en.wikipedia.org/wiki/Dropa_stones.

15. "Nicholas Roerich," Wikipedia, last modified Jan. 21, 2108, https://en.wikipedia.org/wiki/Nicholas_Roerich.

16. R. W. Bernard, "Agharta, the Subterranean World," Biblioteca

Pleyades (website), accessed Jan. 29, 2018, www.bibliotecapleyades .net/tierra_hueca/tierrahueca/chapter7-2.htm.

17. "Lobsang Rampa," Wikipedia, last modified Jan. 28, 2018, https:// de.wikipedia.org/wiki/Lobsang_Rampa.

18. Zecharia Sitchin, *The Cosmic Code* (Rochester, Vt.: Bear & Co., 2002), 42.

CHAPTER 6. ARE THE ANUNNAKI STILL HERE?

1. "ET Disclosure: The Phil Schneider Legacy," American Patriot Friends Network (website), www.apfn.org/apfn/phil.htm; accessed Jan. 24, 2018. Also William Cooper, *Behold a Pale Horse* (Flagstaff, Ariz.: Light Technology, 1991), available as a PDF at Ephrayim (blog), posted Oct. 24, 2010, https://ephraiyim.word press.com/2010/10/24/behold-a-pale-horse-milton-william-cooper -pdf, and Hour of the Time (website), www.hourofthetime.com /wordpresstest/wp-content/uploads/2010/09/William_Cooper -Behold_a_Pale_Horse1991A.pdf; accessed Jan. 29, 2018; Also see "Fritz Springmeier," Wikipedia, last modified Dec. 12, 2017, https:// en.wikipedia.org/wiki/Fritz_Springmeier; see "Fritz Springmeier: Trauma Based Mind Control, Illuminati's Anti-Human Agenda," Springmeier's book about mind control, written with Cisco Wheeler: *The Illuminati Formula Used to Create an Undetectable Total Mind Controlled Slave,* available at the Christian Observer website: http:// hisheavenlyarmies.com/documents/the-illuminati-formula-used-to -create.pdf; accessed Jan. 24, 2018.

2. Anthony F. Sanchez, *UFO Highway* (e-book, www.UFOHighway .com, 2010). No longer available for download (allegedly censored). Cf. Guido Fox, "Linda Moulton Howe and Anthony Sanchez: Secret History of the Progenitors and Anunnaki," video, posted Nov. 21, 2014, www.youtube.com/watch?v=TlL8eB1ZNQ0#t=171; and The Cosmos News, "Edward Snowden: UFOs Come from

Ultra-Terrestrial Civilization in Earth Mantle," video, posted July 17, 2013; www.youtube.com/watch?v=9Ytz3hFh2-U#t=26, all accessed Feb 8, 2018.

3. Ephraim Batambuse III, "'Tall, White' Space Aliens Control America, NSA Leaked Documents Reveal," PC Techmag website, posted Jan. 14, 2014, http://pctechmag.com/2014/01/tall -white-space-aliens-control-america-nsa-leaked-documents-reveal; "Space Aliens Control America Says Snowden," Help Free the Earth (website), Jan. 2014; www.helpfreetheearth.com/news989 _AliensMoney.html; Nemesis Maturity (website), "Snowden Documents Proving 'Alien/Extraterrestrial Intelligence Agenda' Is Driving US Gov Since 1945," video, posted Jan. 24, 2014, www.youtube.com/watch?v=Ur0LNT34MFk; and Sorcha Faal, "Snowden Documents Proving 'US-Alien-Hitler' Link Stuns Russia," What Does It Mean (website), posted Jan. 11, 2014, www .whatdoesitmean.com/index1730.htm.

4. David McCormack, "Aliens Already Walk among Us and Are Refusing to Share Their Technology Until We Change Our Warring and Polluting Ways, Claims Former Canadian Defense Minister," *The Daily Mail* (website), Jan. 8, 2014, www.dailymail.co.uk/news /article-2535698/Aliens-walk-theyre-refusing-share-technology -change-warring-polluting-ways-claims-former-Canadian -defense-minister.html; Evolution Television, "Alien Contact— Canadian Defence Minister—Disclosure 2014?" video, posted Sept. 2, 2013, www.youtube.com/watch?v=2xINSwvNx1A#t=16; "UFO Disclosure of Aliens Revealed," video, The Spottydog Reviews (website), posted Feb. 11, 2014, www.youtube.com /watch?v=UmoSTXRzsoM; and We Are Change (website), "The Highest Ranking Politician That Believes in Aliens," video, Jan. 30, 2015, www.youtube.com/watch?v=T5mkunE_g9U&x-yt-cl =85114404&x-yt-ts=1422579428.

5. "*Equilibrium* (Film)," Wikipedia, last modified Feb. 1, 2018, https://en.wikipedia.org/wiki/Equilibrium_%28film%29.

6. Preston James, Secret Space War series, available at Veterans Today (website): www.veteranstoday.com/?s=%22secret+space+war%22 &x=7&y=2; accessed Jan. 25, 2018; and Alien Agenda, multiple articles available at Veterans Today, www.veteranstoday.com/?s=%22alien+Agenda%22&x=8&y=3; accessed Jan. 25, 2018.

7. Wes Penre, "The Wes Penre Papers," available at the Wes Penre website; http://wespenre.com; accessed Jan. 25, 2018.

8. "Evil from the Heavens," Christian Reincarnation (website); www.christian-reincarnation.com/PDF/Evheav.pdf; accessed Jan. 25, 2018.

9. Barbara Marciniak, *Bringers of the Dawn: Teachings from the Pleiadians* (Rochester, Vt.: Bear & Co., 1992).

10. "Raëlism," Wikipedia, last modified Nov. 15, 2017, https://en.wikipedia.org/wiki/Ra%C3%ABlism.

11. "Did Raël Meet Anunnaki?" Christian Reincarnation (website), www.christian-reincarnation.com/RaelAn.htm; accessed Jan. 25, 2018.

12. Brian Greene, *The Hidden Reality: Parallel Universes and the Deep Laws of the Cosmos* (New York: Knopf, 2011). See also "The Hidden Reality," Wikipedia, last modified Sept. 16, 2017, https://en.wikipedia.org/wiki/The_Hidden_Reality.

13. "Separation Has Begun," Revolutionizing Awareness (website), http://revolutionizingawareness.com/category/the-esoteric-agenda-of-humanity/messages-from-emmanuelle-by-langa, accessed Jan. 25, 2018; also "The Separation has Begun," Biblioteca Pleyades, posted March 25, 2010, www.bibliotecapleyades.net/ciencia/ciencia_consciousuniverse46.htm.

14. Paul Begley, "NASA ORION Will Save Mankind," posted Dec. 5, 2014, www.youtube.com/watch?v=bcXSALuqmZM#t=276; "Project Orion: Nuclear Propulsion," Wikipedia, last modified Jan. 22, 2018, https://en.wikipedia.org/wiki/Project_Orion_%28nuclear_propulsion%29; and Watcher Meet-Up web forum, http://watchermeet-up.forumotion.com/t10592-nasa-orion-will-save-mankind-colonies-mars-moon-space; accessed Jan. 25, 2017.

15. Leslie Watkins, *Alternative 3* (London: Sphere, 1978). This has been long out of print but has been republished as *Alternative 3: Thirty-Third Anniversary Edition* (Nantwich, England: Archimedes, 2010). This version is also available here: https://archive.org/details/Alternative3-33rdAnniversaryEdition. Cf. "The Elite Chose 'Alternative 3,'" Biblioteca Pleyades (website), www.bibliotecapleyades.net/exopolitica/esp_exopolitics_ZK.htm; accessed Jan. 25, 2018.

16. Rory Cellan-Jones, "Stephen Hawking Warns Artificial Intelligence Could End Mankind," BBC News (website), Dec. 2, 2014, www.bbc.com/news/technology-30290540.

17. "'Summoning the Devil': Elon Musk Warns against Artificial Intelligence," RT (website), posted Oct. 27, 2014, http://rt.com/usa/199863-artificial-intelligence-dangers-humanity; and "Elon Musk: Artificial intelligence Will Be 'More Dangerous than Nukes,'" RT, Aug. 4, 2014, http://rt.com/usa/177900-musk-artificial-intelligence-nukes.

18. John C. Lilly, *The Scientist: A Metaphysical Autobiography,* 2nd ed. (Berkeley, CA: Ronin, 1997), 148 ff.

19. Lilly, *The Scientist,* 149.

20. Ray Kurzweil, *The Age of Spiritual Machines: When Computers Exceed Human Intelligence* (New York: Viking, 1999).

21. Ananda W. P. Guruge, "The Buddha's Encounter with Mara the Tempter," Access Insight (website), 2005, www.accesstoinsight.org/lib/authors/guruge/wheel419.html.

22. Jan Erik Sigdell, *Wiedergeburt und frühere Leben* [Rebirth and past lives] (Hanau, Germany: Amra, 2015), appendix.

23. Alfred Lambremont Webre, "Mark Passio: Transforming the Satanic Elements in Human Consciousness," video, posted Sept. 24, 2014, https://www.youtube.com/watch?v=q4DQqla-q74; and Dismantle the Matrix, "Mark Passio Demolishes the Fake-Ass 'Christian' Morons," video posted Feb. 7, 2015; www.youtube.com/watch?v=dWXGo7Qkr2w#t=31.

24. Evilindustrydotcom, "Katy Perry Says She Sold Her Soul to the Devil," video, posted May 17, 2010, www.youtube.com/watch?v =10rx15v28yk.

25. Gregg Prescott: "How To Exit The Reincarnation System," http://howtoexitthematrix.com/2016/10/28/how-to-exit-the -reincarnation-system, accessed Feb. 12, 2018; and Wes Penre: "Do Not Enter the Tunnel," video, posted Nov. 14, 2016, www .youtube.com/watch?v=FUz-BfAKo3k, and "They Recycle Your Soul," video, posted July 29, 2017, www.youtube.com /watch?v=QO3R167Br1o.

ABOUT THE AUTHOR

Jan Erik Sigdell, born in Sweden, holds a doctorate in medical engineering. He has written a number of articles about electronics and the application of technology in medicine and has developed a mathematical theory for mass transfer in a hollow-fiber dialyzer. He lived in Switzerland for thirty years and since 1997 has lived in Slovenia, his wife's home country. In the 1970s, he experimented with hypnotic past-life regressions, and since 1980 he has also practiced nonhypnotic regression therapy. In relation to this, he researched extensively in texts and scriptures about the relationship between Christianity and reincarnation as a frequent visitor to various European university libraries. This gradually expanded to an interest in the history of religion in general, to later include ancient Mesopotamian texts and their relationship to the Bible.

INDEX

Page numbers in *italics* indicate illustrations.